It Will Rain

It Will Rain

a book of essays

Dina Kucera

Copyright © 2015 Dina Kucera

All rights reserved. No part of this publication may be reproduced or transmitted in any form or by any means, electronic or mechanical, including photocopying, recording, or any information storage and retrieval system, except for brief quotations in critical articles and reviews, without the prior written permission of the author.

Kucera, Dina.
It Will Rain : a book of essays / Dina Kucera
p. cm.
ISBN 978-1511997218
1. Kucera, Dina–Mental health. 2. Depressed persons–United States–Family relationships. 3. Depression–United States–Biography. 4. Biography & Autobiography–United States–Personal Memoirs. 5. Family & relationships–United States–Parenting. 6. Humor–United States–Essays. I. Title.

Editor: Julia Lee Bristow
Cover & book design: Julia Lee Bristow
Cover photo: John Wilhelm

This book is for my mom and dad, with huge love and gratitude…

Contents

Prelude
1

It Will Rain
3

Suck It Up
5

Big Yellow Bus
17

Mom
23

Huey
25

Arrested Development
31

Filthy Beggars
41

Lawn Art
47

Thirty-six
55

Travel in Poverty
69

Deepak
79

Loco Anna
89

Five Minutes
105

If I Could Turn Back Time
109

Mr. Bojangles
113

Dear Dr. Phil
117

Heaven
121

Little Cakes
131

Happy Ending
137

Combat Boots
149

A Letter to Me
151

Acknowledgments

When you're an author and you're rolling down the street with your ninth grade education, it's important to find someone educated and brilliant to assist. Thank you, Julia Lee Bristow, for editing, patience, and making people believe that I am also educated and brilliant.

Thank you, John Wilhelm, for your talent and creativity in taking the cover photograph for this book.

Thank you to my husband John, and my daughters, Jennifer, April, and Carly, for bringing me food and snacks while I slept for eight months.

Thank you, Mike O'Mary, for being a friend and teacher.

And thank you my two grandsons, Moses and Matthew… Not for telling me how wonderful the world is, but by showing me how wonderful the world is.

Prelude

I'm much stronger and much smarter, and I can see you sparkling in the night sky like a diamond, side-by-side with other people who got left behind. Other people who also feel invisible, but in reality, we all light up the sky with brilliant, beautiful color.

It Will Rain

Every day, I take a step further and further from the world, from my family, my life, everything, and everyone. Every day, I turn away from reality and truth, and take another step toward the end of the earth. My memories are screaming, but the pounding rhythm of my heartbeat in my ears thankfully drowns out the details.

My view of life is gray and interaction with others creates numbness. I watch people talking or laughing, but I can't hear anything. It's like watching an old black and white movie with static and crackling as the film rolls.

As I take another step out of my life, I reach a place where I step off the edge of the earth. It's not a place I would like to take my life. It's a place where there is no vision, air, or sound. A step off the edge of Earth is a feeling of relief, because when I take that step, there is nothing. No sadness, feeling, thought, or pain. Just nothingness.

Watching from that place, while everyone else is on solid ground, there is no memory of my time as a participant. It's just me. Free falling

My heart, mind, spirit, soul.... If at least one of these things is still dangling by a thread, I have a chance. But as each thread breaks, one at a time, I can feel them physically leaving, creating a huge space that I can't fill.

People tell me I have so much. They tell me that so many people love me. But I'm not connected to people; I'm not connected to myself. I see their lips moving and all I hear are letters that make words that make a sentence. It's numbing. There's no color or weather or time. Yellow and purple and the rain and the sun—they are all one thing blended together to create gray.

If I say the words, "I am worth fighting for," even if I don't really believe, it's something. Even if I am only hanging by that fragile thread, it's something—instead of nothing. I can see land from where I am, treading water in the middle of the ocean. It feels impossible, but I have to fight for my life. That's the only way to escape nothingness.

My heart is heavy, my spirit is heavy, but the journey will hopefully lead me to solid ground. I want to *want* to be here. I want to laugh and cry and open my arms and embrace the beauty in life that I'm told is hiding from me in plain sight. I want to step into the sun. Because until I do, it will rain.

Suck It Up

I waited a long time to write a book that was nonstop hilarity. I believed eventually all the insanity would become funny, easy, and with no trauma, and we would all become a deliriously happy family. I would create a legacy of inspiration and brilliance with zero effort on my part. The knowledge would come organically, naturally. I would be inspired just by being around myself. Then I would write a four-hundred-page book with long lists of things that I'd learned.

I waited for this ocean of knowledge, but every day that passed, I actually became dumber than I was the day before. Is it possible that this powerful knowledge was eluding me as I lay on the couch watching *The Housewives*? Now, as I edit what I know for sure, it's only about four things, and three of those things are negative facts about my husband. Nothing negative about me, but a long list of ways *he* could improve.

My office was also the junk room of the house. Someone put an old desk on the street, which means, if you want this broken-down desk, take it away. So I did. My faded, old brown desk sat against a wall next to a window in a back bedroom. I would stare out at the weather-beaten storage shed overflowing with garbage and Bud Light cans as the mini blinds moved in rhythm with the air-conditioning. Surrounded by boxes of junk, old toys, box-upon-box of things that no one would claim, unless, of course, I suggested the stuff be thrown out.

The highlight of my day was sitting in my hoarder office with the door shut and locked because on the other side were my people.

My husband John with a bandage around his entire head because he had a tumor removed from his neck. He had to sleep sitting up and I was reminded of this every three seconds. He was given specific instructions by the surgeon to keep the thick bandage around his head for seven days. Five days in, I walked into my bathroom and the bandage was sitting on the counter and John was walking around like Tony Soprano on heavy pain medication, "I don't need no fucking bandage." Then he attempted to high-five me as I walked out of the room.

My daughter, April, has to give her fourteen-year-old son Moses his seizure medication twice a day because he has about ten little seizures a day. April is under relentless stress.

The complexity of caring for a child with special needs is mind-blowing. Moses has cerebral palsy and autism and he can erupt into a full-blown meltdown at any second. The last time I tried to intervene, he broke two of my ribs.

My mother's mind had been completely drained by dementia and Parkinson's disease. She had about one hundred television series' DVDs and when I would open her door, I would see empty DVD cases discarded on her bedroom floor. She would have removed all the DVDs and placed them on her bed and then sit paralyzed not knowing how they got there. She did this three or four times a week. She couldn't remember taking them out and couldn't match the correct disk to the correct case. So she would sit on her walker, frozen, scanning the blanket of disks wondering what she was supposed to do next. I always had to hide my frustration.

What was once humorous became infuriating. Mom would take all the clothing from her drawers and off the hangers and put them in a giant mound in the middle of the floor.

She would sit on her walker in her bathroom to put on makeup—eyeliner on her lips, mascara on her eyebrows, and lipstick on her cheeks. She would cut her own hair. She announced one day that it was her "civil right" to have a pair of scissors in her room. She had Parkinson's disease, which meant her hands and arms shook out of control, so when she cut her own hair, it would be possible for her to end up with stitches in her ear or an eye patch.

I would make the turn into her bathroom to find hair on the floor and makeup everywhere—I mean everywhere—on the counter, mirror, floors, and of course, on her face. I would be momentarily startled. She would announce, "I want to be wearing my makeup when I go to heaven. When will that happen?" I would tell her it would happen when she had finished all the things God had planned for her.

She once told me a family member informed her she would not get into heaven if she accepted that my daughter was gay. Mom said she was told she should be trying to "save" her with the words of Jesus and if she wasn't doing this, she would not go to heaven. She asked if I thought it was true.

When I heard things like this, which I had my entire life, it always created instant rage. Here was an old, sick woman, who could pass away at any time. My mother had lived a certain way her whole life with the goal of having her soul saved by Jesus so she could live in heaven for eternity. I didn't know if I personally believed that, but I would never, ever question my mother's beliefs. *Ever.* So when she asked me this as I swept up the hair on the floor, I told her I did not believe it was true, as my stomach churned with anger. I guaranteed she would go to heaven and the person who gave her this information probably would not.

In the evenings, Mom had anxiety attacks, so she was prescribed Klonopin. She usually tried to refuse the pill because she was afraid to become "a strung-out drug addict." Possibly, her habit would get so out of control she would turn into a prostitute and start asking people for spare change in front of a 7-Eleven. I said that she was seventy-seven and she was not only *allowed* to get addicted to pills, but it was *encouraged*. I explained that all senior citizens take pills, gamble, and get drunk, and about how much I am looking forward to being an old drunk lady asleep in my chair, drooling and clutching a lottery scratch ticket.

Mom was miserable, unhappy, and sick. I could be in a grocery store or a restaurant, and clearly hear my mom crying or mumbling, even when she wasn't with me. She couldn't talk, walk, or think. I spent a majority of my time *with* my mom searching *for* my mom.

Over the years, it had been a rocky road with me and the girls, and with John having a heart attack and getting tumors. I had endured a steady stream of calls and visits from mental hospitals, detoxes, jails, police departments, and at least one family member had been in every hospital in the city of Phoenix. I wasn't a victim in any way. I had caused my share of insanity within the walls of our home. Me, John, the girls, we had all contributed to sustaining the Titanic. Every time it surfaced, one of us ran it into another iceberg.

I know most things heal with time. That's what happened to us. Time passed and everyone in my family seemed to be getting better—getting well—and everything had calmed down.

My mother's condition deteriorated, but John and I and the girls got better. I had a moment to breathe and think, and to have some feelings about things that had happened that I was unable to reflect on during the time of actual events.

During those times, I didn't have the luxury of falling apart. I had to power through to make things happen. I had to be strong, to move and think quickly, and that's what I did. I look back and remember the insanity and chaos and I don't know how I made it down the road as far as I did.

I was proud that I had not been crushed under the weight of it all. I had never done anything in my life I was proud of. I was the embodiment of low self-esteem. I looked around with complete surprise and pride that all three of my daughters were still alive. I didn't do it, they did. But to this day, it's remarkable they are all alive.

I didn't pay a ton of attention to the fact that my night terrors never stopped. Or that my anxiety was always present on a low burn. I thought we were all finally coming out on the other end, so my physical and emotional scarring would eventually fizzle out.

It was a time of celebration. Our family was in one piece and learning to talk and laugh together. I looked forward to the family gatherings, the grandsons running around, the girls lying by the pool, John cooking hot dogs on the grill. It was like the sun came out. We were all here. I was thankful to God that we had escaped serious repercussions like prison or death.

A doctor recommended wine for John's heart condition, so he took full advantage of that medical advice. John, staggering around the house because according to him, wine is good for his heart. John is not fun if he drinks too much wine and I can freely say this because John doesn't read books. Even his wife's books. Hilarious, right? I can say anything. The point is, we made it to the other side. And I was finally happy.

It was very quiet in my life. One day, for no apparent reason, I felt a little bit sad, overwhelmed, in over my head. I had a childhood memory pop into my mind, as it had many times before. It always made me feel anxiety until I could force it out of my head.

I had an experience when I was sixteen that involved a sexual interaction with a priest and this unsolicited memory would enter my head every couple of months. I could easily shake it away. It was never a lasting emotional issue of any kind.

The memory of this encounter always caused an inexplicable physical reaction. It felt like when the sky suddenly becomes dark and you hear that first crackling of thunder. The sharp noise hits your stomach and causes it to turn over.

This day, the event entered my head accompanied by the sudden darkness and the clap of thunder jolting my stomach, and the memory garnered the usual shift to thinking about something else, which was always the cure and a method that worked one hundred percent of the time.

I'm a firm believer that a nap cures most things, so I lay down and told John to wake me in one hour. An hour passed, then another hour. For whatever chemical, emotional, or spiritual reason, I was unable to get out of bed. I was unable to turn off this experience from so, so long ago. It did not leave my head and I couldn't stop it. I began to cry and didn't stop. For months. I lay in bed for eight months.

Like most people, I have some horrible memories, but most of the memories I have from my childhood are beautiful and funny. Memories of a time when I was a

IT WILL RAIN

young girl laughing with great friends and running the dirt roads smoking our parents' cigarettes. Who wants to read an entire book about depression? Not me. So I'm hoping that I am able to sprinkle this book with a little bit of laughter and hope. The things in life that are funny are more valuable than the sad memories, in my opinion.

The only comforts for me ever, depressed or not, are the hilarious memories from my life. Laughter and the pursuit of what's funny has always been the thing that has saved my life. Without laughter, I know I would not be here. Without laughter, life, as far as I'm concerned, is not worth living.

I have always believed people with depression are weak-minded people. I had never been able to "clock-out" of my life and be depressed. The mantra in my head has always been, "Suck it up. Carry on cry baby." Then, I literally could not get out of bed for eight months.

When you're depressed, you hear things like this all the time: "You've got to go do something! You have to make yourself feel better!" All the suggestions are meant to help and encourage, but my brain was not open to this repetitive, annoying, nails-on-a-chalkboard information.

One thing I have found to be intolerable my entire life is people feeling sorry for themselves. I do it every now and again; I think we all do. This didn't feel like that. I lay in my bed and said to myself, I have a great life. I have an amazing husband and three beautiful daughters. What's wrong with me?

At my worst, I thought, If I could just put my socks on. It took every ounce of energy I had to put on my socks because all I did was lie in bed. I didn't move enough for my blood to circulate, so my feet were always frozen. I'd put one sock on, lie down. An hour later, put the other sock on.

Every morning, I immediately felt overwhelmed with sadness and it worsened as the hours passed. Most mornings, I would wake up and begin to cry ten seconds after opening my eyes. My heart felt broken. Every day I wondered, How long is this going to last?

I could see my mother in my head: her constant, violent shaking because of the Parkinson's disease and dementia, the unending hallucinations. Still, my mom prayed every single day, so I wonder where God was while all this was going on. Why couldn't he hear her? Is this God's will?

I thought about my daughters, Jennifer, April, and Carly, and all the pain they have experienced. I thought about my husband John and his heart condition. I thought about my grandson, Moses, and his daily seizures. Where was God?

In my life, I was always able to turn to God. It didn't matter what was going on, God was there with me. Most of the time, he was shaking his head saying, "Really Dina? Did you just do that?" But God always stuck by me.

The fact is, I had never been open to *feeling* my feelings. I didn't like having negative feelings. About anything. If I couldn't fix it, it didn't happen. I would walk away.

That's what society taught us, right? If you were strong, you could simply walk away from whatever traumatic things happened to you. That was my definition of strength. Then I found myself broken in half and realized that strength was actually the opposite. Strength turned out to be looking in the eyes of horror and not backing down from it even when filled with fear.

The "pretend-it-never-happened" method will, at some point, give you a nervous breakdown; although, I prefer it to being that person who has feelings about everything. They feel the feelings and want to feel more about how

IT WILL RAIN

they feel about the feelings. Okay man. I get it. You have some feelings. Damn.

I have, at times, needed days or several days to mentally unravel in order to become emotionally healthy. But I ignored the demons, because of my strength, and hung onto the mental trash I needed to let go of. Most of the things that filled my head were completely useless to me. So I walked around the world carrying my big bag of useless shit. People would say, "What's that awful smell?" I would cheerfully respond, "Oh. That's my giant bag of shit. I take it everywhere." I expected that if someone loved me enough they would actually hold my bag of shit for me.

So what I learned to do was ignore my feelings. So I didn't get to choose where I would randomly be forced to feel something. That sets up a situation where I leave my unaddressed feelings to present themselves at any time. The deli counter at the grocery store is the perfect place to reflect on that thing that happened when I was ten.

I could be standing in Target and someone could walk by who looks like, or smells like, or laughs like… and here we go… an enormous flood of feelings begin snowballing downhill. You're standing there like a normal, strong person holding a bottle of Windex, sobbing uncontrollably as people stare at you. Most women understand this, so they watch you and whisper to one another, "She's having a feeling. God bless her. I had a feeling in Sizzler last week."

I traveled a long road without having feelings, so I know it can be done. But if you do that, just know that one of these days, you're going to be in Macy's and all hell is going to break loose. To be honest, I don't think a person is truly authentic until they have an emotional breakdown in public.

I'm a horrible mother. That was one of the large pieces of shit that I carried in my bag. But I had to be careful not to live in the "I'm a bad mother" world because the kids would use that to attack me like a pack of wolves.

"Mom. Will you babysit for me?"
"No, I just don't feel very well."
"My childhood was bad."
"Okay. Bring him over."

They would allow me to carry their mistakes by saying that they made them because of the horror that was their childhood. "I am the way I am because of the way you raised me." Yes, I will hold your bag of shit.

Days turned into weeks and weeks turned into months. I stopped showering, brushing my teeth, and I never changed out of my pajamas. John, Jennifer, April, and Carly were losing their patience. They had taken such great care of me; they had been kind and loving, but eventually they were done with it.

They would peak their heads into my bedroom door and say, "You okay?" The older girls would drag their sons in by the collars and say, "Give your grandmother a kiss." There's Grandma; hadn't done my roots for God knows how long, hadn't showered. My hair was actually starting to form dreadlocks. I looked like a white, old-lady version of Flavor Flav. "Give Grandma a kiss God dammit!" The sweet boys gave me a kiss.

The grandsons were also tired of it. They wanted me back in the kitchen making chocolate milk and macaroni and cheese. They were ready for life to return to normal. But I believe by that point I had already stepped off the edge of the earth. I was immersed in complete silence.

Depression came over me like someone dumped water on my head and it rolled all the way down to my feet. Sometimes people what they call "situational depression." That's when you have something traumatic happen in your

IT WILL RAIN

life and, as a result, you become depressed. Then there is the depression I was in. Where there is no apparent reason. One day I just climbed into bed and didn't get out until I had dreadlocks.

I say there is no *apparent* reason because I learned there is almost always a reason. If you are depressed there is something, some day, or some memory you have ignored. Because you're "strong."

I think most people have a day they are trying to forget and that day drives us to alcohol, drugs, mental wards, and homelessness. So when I see someone on the streets and they look completely broken down, I wonder what they are trying to forget. What memory are they desperately trying to remove from their heads? It's something horrible enough that they would rather die than to think or talk about it.

Even average people have things in their heads they have to shake away. The nice young girl at the bank. The man who does your taxes. The person sitting next to you in church. These are people whose hearts are consumed with memories that they will run from to their death. They are rudderless and spiritually numb, all the way to the psych ward, jail, or the morgue.

So we try to escape the images or words that fill our heads and our hearts with brief moments of peace when we drink or drug or shop or eat. During these activities the memory fades and there is a sense of calm—a feeling of safety. But it's always temporary; the memory comes back and we begin to run again. We run all the way down the road with our giant, useless bag of shit.

I told John this book was about feelings. After he signed the release form I said, "You want to read it? A hundred-and-something pages packed with feelings." He said, "Well. Not really. But I'm sure it's great." It is great, John. It is.

Big Yellow Bus

One of the most menial jobs I had is also one of the best memories I have about my mom. My mother and I delivered papers on a newspaper route together. We had about two hundred and fifty customers so it took about four hours. She was normal and healthy, the opposite of the condition she's in now. I was physically fit and clear-headed, the opposite of the condition I'm in now.

The papers arrived in our driveway in big bundles with an elastic band holding each bundle together. We loaded the bundles of newspapers and the babies into the backseat and before we backed out of the driveway, we wrapped about seventy-five papers. When we finished wrapping the papers, our hands would be black with ink and then we would proceed to touch our face and pick up the babies throughout the four-hour period.

It was pointless to say, "Hey, you have black all over your face." Having black ink all over your face was part of the job. Having babies covered in black ink was also part of the job.

An hour or so into the paper route, I would go into a convenience store to get a drink and, somehow, I would always run into some popular giggling girls from high school. I dropped out in the ninth grade so I could take care of my babies—because I was a good mom/child.

The girls would whisper to one another, giggle, and one of them would say, "Hey, you have black all over your face."

I would say, "Yeah, I know." Then I would stare at them while taking a sip of the straw, holding my ground ... and my baby. It was my way of saying, "I can't be shamed. I'm proud of my work. Without me, you would not have your TV Guide." Of course, on the inside I was dying as they would jump into their shiny Trans Am with their clean, buttery Latina skin, and I would watch them drive off with Parliament on full blast.

We folded and wrapped newspapers with thick rubber bands as we drove. Then we would roll up to a house or trailer and I would throw the paper out of my window with the strength of an Olympic athlete. From my parked van on the street, I could throw a paper all the way across the yard, over the broken-down cars, with unbelievable accuracy and make it land right at the screen door.

I'm not sure why, because I only weighed about eighty pounds, but God gave me arms like cannons. If my mom was driving, we didn't even have to stop at the house. As we drove at about forty miles an hour, I could put half my body out of the van window, throw the paper, and still make it land on the porch of a house that was still two houses away. It was a thrill. To me, this was fun. Yes, I'd rather have been driving around in that pretty Trans Am listening to Parliament, but throwing a newspaper the length of a mini mall was a close second.

During this time, my father had a bigger paper route that was from midnight to about six o'clock in the morning. There were several times one of us kids would have to drive for him because he was inebriated. It's a clear memory of driving in the darkness and smelling the alcohol as Dad rambled about things that didn't make sense.

IT WILL RAIN

One time as I took my turn at the wheel, my father leaned forward, visually scanning the dark neighborhood, and then he said, "Stop right here." Before I could stop him, he threw the paper with whatever drunken strength he had without realizing his window was rolled up, making the rolled-up paper violently hit the window and bounce back to the driver's seat, hitting me in the head. As I sat up trying to regain my equilibrium, my dad was still leaning forward staring out his window. He said, "I don't even know where that went."

Mom and I talked and laughed the entire four hours, Monday through Saturday. We talked about love and life and everything that's funny. We knew most of the people to whom we delivered papers, which would instigate a thirty-minute assessment of each customer and their children and the crimes they had committed. In the area I grew up, there was no shortage of people that were in jail, waiting to go to jail, or hiding from jail.

One completely broken-down house that we delivered to belonged to an older couple who began drinking early in the morning, so by the time we came around to deliver their paper, one of them would be staggering around their dirt front yard having a conversation with their barking pit bull "Loco" that was chained to a metal pole.

You could hear the intoxicated woman screaming at the dog, "Loco! What about being a good boy for mommy?" I don't think Loco had any intention of being a good boy for mommy. The lady stood there smoking a cigarette, and I noticed her bright red nails were so long they were actually curling. She'd take a drag of her cigarette and the red nails would touch her chin. Her eyebrows were not-so-carefully drawn in black on her forehead, so it made her look like she was in a constant state of surprise.

One day, we stopped in front of this house at ten thirty in the morning. The man was standing in the front yard already intoxicated as Loco violently jumped and barked, scowling and grinding his teeth, staring at the old man. Then we noticed there was a giant yellow school bus parked on the side of the house.

It was very common for many of our customers to want to chitchat with us as we delivered their paper. So instead of throwing the paper, I reached my arm out my window, smiling, and handed him his paper. This old man had long jet-black hair that was always combed back with some kind of grease and pulled into a ponytail. It was so greasy it was shiny.

He smiled and looked absolutely giddy, "What do you think? I bought a bus!"

Mom and I said something to the effect of, "Wow, it's big. There's always some kind of occasion where you need an enormous bus," and, "We wish we had a bus."

He proudly smiled at the giant yellow eyesore and then was abruptly shaken out of his dream state by his violent dog, "Loco! Be a good boy and daddy will give you a chicken!"

The very next day, as we drove up the dirt road, we saw him standing in his front yard. We pulled up and again I smiled and handed him his paper. He was even more intoxicated on this day.

He walked over to my window and said, "She left me. She wanted me to choose between her and the bus." Then we saw Loco in the bus jumping violently, running back and forth with part of a green bus seat in his mouth. He screamed, "Loco! Daddy bought you a bus!" Then he looked at us trying to hide his humiliation as he took a giant, angry drag off his cigarette, "I don't care. All my life I've dreamed of having a bus and now I have one."

Mom and I said something like, "You can't break a person's dream; dreams are like food; you could use your dreams as a pillow."

The next day we were coming down the street, the bus was gone, and the man and the lady were standing in the front yard like they had just come home from a honeymoon in Juarez. Loco was sitting in the dirt chewing on a steering wheel—a large steering wheel—much like the ones they have in buses.

The man walked over to my window, I handed him his newspaper and he sort of whispered, "My lady came home. I sold the bus to my cousin, you know, he has eight kids."

Mom and I said something like, "Love always wins," or, "Love is more powerful than air."

Pivotal moment. Any time in our life we feel we are above, or better, than another human being, God personally reminds us not to pass judgment on other people. This man actually looked at me and said, "You have something black on your face."

We waved goodbye and began our journey down the road. I got back in the zone—my perfectly wrapped newspapers flying through the air and landing exactly where I wanted them to fall.

I was a teenager with two babies and a paper route, and I remember being really happy during that time.

It's interesting to me that I had so little and didn't even think about wanting more. I was content in my small world, never having a need or desire to see the giant world that was outside my little bubble—ink-stained face and hands, cute babies, driving down the dirt roads with Earth, Wind and Fire on full blast—I was simple. Man, have times changed.

Mom

My mother never had the luxuries in life. She never once went on vacation. She never had fancy clothes and she never smelled of perfume or flowery lotion.

Did she ever dream she was a ballerina, gliding across a wooden floor, toes pointed, and hands gently waving across the air as if she were playing an invisible harp? Her hair gathered perfectly on top of her head with a coat of pink lipstick, as she softly twirled, feeling grateful to be a ballerina....

Did she ever imagine what it would be like to paint a picture of places she had never seen? A painting of an ocean under a foggy sky, with the touch of her hand creating the waves in a way that makes people think water is coming in on them just by looking at it. And she would know in her heart she had been to these places because she was an artist....

Did she dream of standing on a stage lit only by tea lights, singing a song about broken hearts in a beautiful white gown that rolled down her legs into a puddle of cloth on the ground around her feet? Looking into the eyes of the people listening because she knew they also had broken hearts and feeling loved because they understood....

Did she dream that she and my father would learn to do the Tango? Or drive up the coastal highway alongside the ocean in a car without a roof, have a candlelit dinner on the rooftop of an old building in New York, hold my father's hand while they ice skated, slow dance to a love song being played by a piano player who understood because he had also been in love....

My mother loved so big that her heart was always broken. She loved without any reserve or any lines drawn in the sand. It never mattered the person's bad behavior or character flaws—she just loved.

My mother's dream was to stand outside of our home surrounded by dirt as the six of us played football, running up and down the street, darting back and forth as dirt filled the air and she felt love and she was grateful. She watched and laughed, standing there with her hands on her hips.

She dreamed of having all these children playing football on the dirt road as she watched cheering for both sides. She dreamed of watching them and loving them. At night when they were all tucked away in bed with scraped knees and a possible broken finger, she dreamed of what would come the following day. Then she would sleep feeling blessed with these dirt-covered children. This was my mother's dream.

Huey

My mother and father took care of my grandfather, my father's father, in our home. My grandfather had Parkinson's disease and dementia. His right hand never stopped shaking and he dragged one foot as he walked.

His name was Huey and he came before Huey Lewis and the News, so he had to live with that terrible name without the rock-star popularity.

You could hear him shifting down the hall—step-drag, step-drag. He also drooled, which in itself isn't a big deal, but the one handkerchief he used to mop his mouth with, that was a problem. For some reason, he didn't want to turn it over to be washed. No, the others that were clean and folded in his top drawer weren't suitable. He only wanted that one, the wet one, that my mother would sneak out of his room, holding by one corner, running, gagging, throwing it in the wash, slamming the lid shut saying, "Oh god," resting her head on the top of the washing machine while still dry-heaving.

He wore so much Old Spice cologne that you could smell it by standing in the front yard. He used some kind of hair grease to comb his hair back, and because of the Parkinson's, his collar also wore a lot of hair grease. He sprayed his underarms for ten minutes with so much Gillette spray deodorant it filled his entire room with a thick fog. I now think it's possible that he didn't have dementia, but combining all those sprays could have made him high and that's why he did the things he did.

Every morning he got dressed for his day in a button-up shirt, dress pants with a belt, and hard black shoes. He didn't go out often because the dementia made him unpredictable, which is a nice way of saying he was out of his mind and he scared people. He didn't scare us; we thought he was hilarious.

When my daughter, Jennifer, was two or three years old, she would eat breakfast every morning with my grandfather. They would sit at the table, a table that only had room for two chairs, and eat breakfast. Every morning Grandpa would say in his shaky voice, "Where's my buddy?"

Jennifer would answer in her baby voice, "I'm here! I'm here!" and she would climb up onto the big chair. The two of them would just sit there in silence eating oatmeal. My grandfather would pull that handkerchief out of his pocket and the only person that didn't double over with nausea was two-year-old Jennifer. If she got a touch of oatmeal on her chin, I could see my grandfather pull out that wet, cloth handkerchief and I would run, screaming, "I got it! Thanks Grandpa, I got it," dabbing Jen's chin with a napkin.

With advanced-stage Parkinson's, my grandfather got to the point where he couldn't talk. It's part of the illness. His voice became very small, reduced to a whisper, and in order to hear what he was saying, you had to put your ear right up to his mouth. So he spoke very little.

One time, he needed a new razor, so I took him to the store and the young man at the counter was my friend Eddie whom I had gone to school with. My grandfather asked how he knew this razor worked. Eddie said, "If it doesn't work, sir, you can bring it back."

IT WILL RAIN

My grandfather opened the package right there at the counter and told Eddie, "Give me your arm." Eddie looked at me and I just shook my head in horror. Eddie laid his hairy arm on the counter and my grandfather took the razor with zero hesitation and shaved a clean line all the way up his arm. Then he said, "That looks good. I'll take it." Eddie began to laugh really hard and said, "I can't believe that just happened." I apologized over and over.

He enjoyed going to the grocery store, although, he never got groceries, but he would get fixated on a particular product that he had to have—like candy. My grandfather always had money and I'm not completely sure how he got it, but he seemed to have more money that anyone I knew.

We would take him to the store and he would ask a cashier for a few paper bags. He would walk—step-drag, step-drag—make his way to the candy aisle and start picking up whole boxes of candy and dumping them into the paper bags. Hundreds of candy bars. He would say, "This is for the kids."

My father would try to tell him he only needed six candy bars. Grandpa always disputed my father's input and said six wasn't enough. People behind us in line would stare as he poured the candy out of the bags on the register belt, angrily rolling their eyes and walking away to find another register.

He would pull the money out of his pocket and drool, handing the wet money to the cashier. My father would try and help him, but he wouldn't allow anyone to touch his money.

He did this with everything he needed or wanted. A cart full to the top of Gillette spray deodorant. Once he wanted watermelons, a cart full of watermelons as my father furiously shook his head because what the hell are we going to do with sixteen watermelons? This store visit, my grandfather didn't pay for the watermelons. My father tried to intervene, but my grandfather just pushed the cart out of the store as employees watched, including Eddie with his shaved arm. Not one person stopped him.

My father loaded my grandfather and the watermelons into the car and went back into the store and paid for them, which made him furious because we didn't have a spare fifty dollars for watermelons. We got home and were carrying the watermelons in the house as my mother looked puzzled saying, "So..." watching more people walking in with watermelons. She continued, "How...?"

My father said, "Sixteen."

My grandfather was generous with his money, but you really had to need that money because by the time he thumbed through it, oh god, the drool. We would wince and grab the dollar by the very edge corner, feeling our stomachs rise up, fighting the nausea so hard that it would make us sweat.

Sometimes he would just offer you a few dollars. Most of the time we would say, "Oh! No! I'm fine. That's okay Grandpa. You keep your money." In our heads praying to Jesus he didn't insist.

None of this was his fault. It was his illness that caused the drooling, but his illness also caused the other things, which gave us a big laugh.

Once we drove up in the driveway and my grandfather was standing next to the tree in the front yard with an axe. We watched for a minute and he swung the axe, barely hitting the tree. My father got out of the car and asked him what he was doing. He said he was cutting the tree down. My father asked why. He said, "Because I don't like it."

He stood in the front yard for several hours next to this tree and he may have hit it with the axe a total of four times. Then he laid the axe down and came into the house. Defeated.

He had to be hospitalized at the VA Hospital for some tests and my father got a call that they lost my grandfather. He didn't die. They just couldn't find him. My father drove down the busy street in front of the hospital and found my grandfather walking down the street. I heard my father say, "Oh my god." No shoes and wearing the hospital gown, open in the back with my grandfather walking down a six-lane street with his bare ass clear as day for all the traffic to see. Later that day when my father told my mother this story, it was a highlight as we all laughed hysterically.

We came home one day and he was lying on the kitchen floor, awake, but just lying there shaking and drooling. The refrigerator door was open and there was an empty container of red chili lying next to him. When he fell, he dropped the chili and you could see a streak of red from the floor all the way up the wall to the ceiling.

We called an ambulance and as they were lifting him onto the gurney, he told my father right in front of them, "Don't let these thieves rob me. Take my wallet."

It wasn't long after that he passed away. The initial injury was a broken hip, but he quickly declined after that. Didn't grease his hair anymore, didn't get dressed up. No more shopping trips.

My grandfather was sick and his illness caused all the inappropriate behavior. But he did break up our otherwise stress-filled life with unintentional comedy.

Either you are laughing or making someone laugh. Then when that stops, what's the point? That may be the secret to life, laughing. Or making people laugh. It fills us with purpose. I think the word "purpose" brings ideas of great jobs or brilliance of some kind. What if life is just about laughing? If you can laugh once each day, you are a success. And if you make someone laugh, you are a bigger success. That should be the new rule.

Arrested Development

I had been in bed for months and every day my heart felt more broken than the day before. I was unable to do anything, including very small things, like blinking. I couldn't stop crying.

I spent months clicking through Netflix and I watched almost every show. One day I was clicking, crying, clicking... I couldn't live this way anymore. This feeling wasn't going away, as a matter of fact, it was getting worse. I had thought about suicide many times over the previous months. Committing suicide would be the easy thing to do and this day the thought consumed me. The thoughts of suicide were relentless. I could not wake up to this feeling even one more day. I couldn't do it. I couldn't feel the hurt anymore.

As I cried, I saw *Arrested Development* listed as one of the shows Netflix felt I should watch. I watched one episode as I cried.

It took a few days, but I watched every episode, one after the other. I can't say I laughed because that wasn't my mood, but I stared at these people doing all these hilarious things. I couldn't stop watching the show. Then, the credits began to roll at the end of the last episode. I turned the TV off. I looked at the socks on my feet then I rolled over and slept for about seven hours.

Later that evening, I took a handful of Mom's Klonopin. It wasn't because *Arrested Development* ended, although, the episode where one of the characters has giant hooks for hands and he is trying to button the back of his mom's dress almost made me want to stay alive.

My daughter took me to the emergency room.

There are long lists of things I've done in my life that I am ashamed of. This is one of them. Huge, huge regret that I put my family through this. I wanted my daughters to believe I could overcome anything. I wanted them to believe I was strong and I could never be broken. Now I've ruined their inaccurate opinion of me. I was a heap, nothing left. Except for my Jamaican heritage.

The following morning, I woke up, and from previous experience, I knew exactly where I was. I was in the psychiatric hospital. I did remember taking the pills. I did remember crying and screaming at my husband. I did remember my daughter telling me she was taking me somewhere. That's all I remember.

I have been in the mental ward three times and all three times, I was diagnosed as being exhausted. If you've never been in a place like this, I will tell you it's heartbreaking. But it is impossible not to see the comedy when you are surrounded by people who are exactly like you.

I stared at the roof. I looked to my left—nothing. I looked to my right—nothing. Rooms in the mental hospital are empty because people will try and kill themselves with anything they can get their hands on. I rolled out of bed, dizzy, still under the influence of god-knows-what, and stumbled to the door.

I walked out into the hallway holding onto the wall and saw a woman at the end of the hall who I later found out was my caseworker. That's what poor people have—caseworkers. The people with good insurance get psychologists with nice offices with picture frames holding degrees from Yale or Harvard and crazy white teeth. I got a caseworker with a giant coffee stain on the front of her scrubs that had brightly colored clown heads all over them.

She saw me coming down the hall and she bent down like you would if you saw a groggy toddler wearing pajamas with feet in them. As I staggered down the hall, she bent down, putting her hands on her knees, cooing, almost in baby talk, "Look who's awake! Look at you! Good for you!"

We got to her cubicle and she was still talking to me like I was a giant baby. I had memory about the night before and began to cry as my head pounded. She looked at me with her enormous social worker smile and said, "Why is Dina sad? Huh? Why are you feeling so sad? Who's sad! Who is sad! I'm going to bite your tummy! I am!" All of the sudden, out of nowhere, I was served a giant plate of sweet baby Jesus.

This lady didn't have one clue who she was dealing with. She said, "We're gonna get you up and running in no time! I see your doctor has prescribed Percocet for your migraines? How bad is your pain right now on a scale of one to ten?"

Zero hesitation and trying to mimic the ten face they have on the pain chart in the doctors' offices. "Eleven."

She said, "I bet. You had a real rough night. I'll go ahead and order that."

Whatever happened in my life before that second, I have no memory of it. As the tears rolled down my face, all I was thinking was, Don't give her a hi-five or hug her. Then she tried to drop a bomb I completely ignored. "Now that medication will be given to you 'as needed.'" To me "as needed" is the same as "I need it."

So every day, psych ward pharmacist and I would do a dance. It was called, "Every time I walk up to this window, you will ask me what my pain level is. I'm going to say ten. You're going to glare at me and shake your head and then you're going to hand me the pills. In ten minutes I'll be feeling well enough to do the Hustle up on the Lido deck."

This part of the mental ward was for women only and I liked that. We had group therapy all day long and weaved into that were kindergarten activities. At first these activities made me feel ridiculous. Did they think we were idiots? But as the days passed I, like any crafty, fun, mentally-ill person, looked forward to them. They became the highlight of my day.

One popular activity was music class. I would run as fast as I could into the music room because there were about twenty drums and only ONE tambourine. I wanted that tambourine, which, in a way, showed my willingness to live. I would sit in the lobby and stare at the clock so I could be first in line, therefore, the first to enter the music room where I would dig to the bottom of the enormous box and pull out the one tambourine.

We got in a huge circle and all the ladies would tap on their drums creating a peaceful, calming, Native American rhythm. I stood down and waited for the appropriate moment to rock the shit out of my tambourine.

The only person I ever heard play the tambourine was Laurie Partridge in the *Partridge Family*. So I pictured her in my mind and I did it the way that she did it. Hip out, boom, and smack the hip. Hand up, boom, and smack the hand. And repeat, over and over.

After a few days of realizing how much I looked forward to the activities, I felt it showed an indication that I was actually backsliding into a state of permanent mental illness. For example, I noticed if we had a lazy activity leader and I felt their activities were not up to par, I would stew in my anger.

When you're in the mental hospital and the activity leader puts zero effort into an activity, it really pisses you off. At least try. A couple of times we would go to the activity room and the caseworker would hand us a piece of paper and tell us to write or doodle for an hour. Are you kidding? Aren't you supposed to think of activities that make us want to stay alive? We would all mumble to one another, "This is lame. What about doing some beading? Or playing some drums? This is fucking bullshit."

Then there was art hour. If I walked around the corner and saw thousands of tiny, sparkly beads in a mound on the table, my heart would absolutely soar. I mean, you can buy this crap in the outside world, but I don't think I'd get much encouragement creating jewelry that only appeals to six-year-olds.

I had Mom, Moses, stress, and depression. I had to act, talk, and feel just the right way, every day, all day. So in the mental hospital nothing was expected of me. All I had to do was be the best six-year-old I could be so there was no way to disappoint anyone. Every day I could feel the weight of life dropping off my shoulders, especially the weight of caring for my mother and the guilt that I felt that way.

We were sitting at a table during art hour, loading our dental floss with sparkly stars and letters. I decided to make my daughter, Jennifer, a beautiful bracelet that simply said "Jennifer." This bracelet would represent my stay in the psych ward.

I began to shovel through all the letters. I couldn't find one single "J," which is an important letter when spelling Jennifer.

Helen (which of course was not her real name because I need to protect the innocent) was one of the patients that you could just tell—she was not going home anytime soon. I really tried to be patient with Helen, but it wasn't easy.

Apparently she didn't have any family, so when the phone rang, Helen answered the phone and talked to any person on the other end. You could walk down the hallway and pass by Helen sitting on a chair talking on the phone and hear her say, "So what are some of your hobbies?" At first I thought she was talking to a family member or friend because she would be laughing really loud, slapping her knee. I would walk back by and hear her say something like, "What kind of dog do you have?"

She would talk on the phone for about twenty minutes and then say, "Dina! Your daughter April is on the phone!" So this is what she did. We only had a certain amount of time to talk on the phone to our family and Helen took up all of our time.

I was still searching for a J when Helen shouted from the end of the table, "Look what I made my cat!" She held up a two-foot long piece of dental floss with about fifty J's on it. Then she said, "Guess what my cat's name is?" We all quietly stared at her. "Jazzy!"

I said, "Why didn't you just spell Jazzy?" And I'm furious. Livid.

Helen shouted, "Because I want it to be a surprise!" There was no point in saying that didn't make any sense. The last thing you wanted to do was get into a back and forth with Helen. In the mental ward.

I think one of the first things caseworkers for psych facilities learn is how to talk in that soft, calming, gentle voice, and if they said what they were thinking it would be, "The sultry sound of my voice will make you want to live." During our activities there was always a caseworker walking around the table encouraging us to stay alive.

I was making Jennifer's bracelet when this particular caseworker circled the table. When she got to me, she leaned down and in her really soft, almost phone-sex voice, she smiled and said, "That is so pretty, Dina. Really. Who you gonna give that to?"

Huh? Who are you gonna give that to? Like I'm an idiot. Like when I get out of this place I hope to have made everyone I love a special kindergarten art project that I made while I was on the brink of insanity. "Here you are Gary. It's a piece of construction paper with cotton balls glued on it." Or, "Here you are mom! I traced my giant adult hand and then I cut it out. Yes! Good eye! I did turn it into a turkey!" Or, "I made you a beautiful bracelet ... Ennifer." Nope. No one will know. What happens on the crazy boat stays on the crazy boat.

I was there for five days when I was called in to an office where two doctors spoke with me. All the above is funny (to me), but the truth is, this depression was killing me. I still couldn't breathe without crying. My enthusiasm for the pain medication only lasted one day.

They asked how I was feeling. I silently stared at them as tears rolled down my face. They asked if I was suicidal and I didn't respond. I just cried. They said my insurance company said I was fine to go home now. They said if I felt like I was not ready to go home, I could prepay the facility three hundred and twenty dollars a day and stay until I was stable. I told them I couldn't afford that. They said it was clear I was still having substantial emotional problems, but there was nothing they could do.

People say, "They can't release you! They have to keep you until you're safe!" Wrong. They can, they will, and they did release me. It happens all day long all across the country. I went home.

I wish I had something really inspiring to say right here. I know people love me and want me and my family to be well and happy. But I can only tell the story the way it happened. Life isn't magic and miracles. That's not to say I haven't had more miracles than I deserve in my life, because I have. But big life problems are never fixed overnight. It's not a fairy tale. It's real life.

I didn't know depression could take over my life. It consumed me. After I got home from the hospital, I climbed back into my bed and I stayed there. For a long, long time. That's what happened. As my husband walked out of the bedroom, in my soft, sexy, caseworker voice I said, "Shut the door."

I think if people saw me out in the world, they would have no idea that I didn't feel well because I looked normal. But because I *wasn't* normal, I would notice other people more than I usually did.

In my head I would come to a conclusion, just by looking at a person, if they were normal or not normal. It always happened in the grocery store because that was the only reason I would leave my room.

I saw a young woman, clearly ravaged by an eating disorder. I felt sad and surprised that she could even walk. Naturally, a thud hit the bottom of my stomach because I wondered if she saw in herself what I saw.

I saw another young man covered in tattoos. I live in Phoenix, so this is fairly common. But this man's entire face and neck were covered in tattoos. He frightened me because even the small glimpse I got, I could see the tattoos weren't flowers; they were violent. It seemed to me to be a road map of his life. At some point this guy was six years old and I wondered, What happened? Why do you hate yourself?

The people that gave me the most fear were the high or intoxicated people either in a public place or staggering

IT WILL RAIN

down the street. I asked myself why I felt such fear when I saw people like this. We all live under the same sky. We're all mixed together carrying the story of how we got to be the people we are today. It's just that some people—I'll include myself in that—we carry our pain with more secrecy. In a more subtle way.

I wonder if for some people, the pain is so great they can't contain it on the inside; does it just boil over and they tell their life story on their skin with tattoos or scars in straight lines from razor blades.

We don't know what people have been through. We don't know what their eyes have seen or how many times their entire world has crashed in around them. These strangers are picking up pizza to feed their kids and then they watch *Law and Order* and they do it all with the memories of the road-map of their life. But when I stand behind them to pick up my pizza, they appear to be completely happy. And normal, if that's still a word.

I've figured out why I fear the anorexic woman and the tattooed man. It's because they are showing the horror that is their life on the outside of their body. It's because I am more *like* them than I am *unlike* them.

I guess I fear my insides will eventually come out on my outside. That should be on the questionnaire at the mental hospital. "Have your insides started to come out on your outside?" If yes, you are admitted.

Filthy Beggars

Mama Lia lived down the street from my grandmother. She was really old, probably in her nineties. She was big on the bottom and wobbled when she walked. She wore bright flower dresses and it seemed like she had an endless number of these dresses, all with a different flower represented.

The houses on my grandmother's street, including my grandmother's and Mama Lia's, were about five hundred square feet. It was as if someone took one large room and put up walls to make it a miniature house.

My cousins, Janelle and Jackie, and I would go visit Mama Lia when we were visiting our grandparents. When we walked through the little white gate in front of her house it was only about two more steps to her screen door. Before we opened the gate, we could see her sitting in her chair and she would see us and scream with excitement. She'd do the thing old, bottom-heavy people do when they try to get off a cushiony chair: rocking and rocking until the momentum of her bottom hurled her into the standing position. She would open the screen door, cheerfully smiling, "There's my girls!"

The three of us would sit facing her on one couch as she talked about people we didn't know. We could care less about these people because we were only in it for a candy bar from the table drawer next to her chair.

Jackie was kind, even as a child, and she actually did care and would ask about the people, which made me and Janelle glare at her because we almost had the candy in our hands when Jackie would say, "How is Barbara's gout?" We would look at Jackie and she would say, "What? She said Barbara had gout." Who is Barbara? What is gout?

After about an hour of hearing about Gail in Lubbock and Frank in Oklahoma City, she would open the drawer and give us our candy bars. It was usually that simple. God forbid she was squabbling with Bernice from Waco or Martha from Deming. We could be there for hours and at some point you don't care about the candy bars, you just want out

Back then that was how old people were. Little kids and their parents didn't have to be afraid of what insane, inappropriate thing they would do. We talked to everyone, including drunken men, and there was never even a hint of impending harm. It was a completely different world. Mama Lia was lonely. She was happy to see us arrive and sad to see us go, running out the screen door with candy bars in our hands.

Aside from visiting old people that our parents and grandparents didn't know, we also walked to the shopping mall. We walked for miles through neighborhoods, one after another; we walked and walked.

Then we would get to the only freeway in Albuquerque at the time, and there was a tall chain-link fence around it so children like us couldn't go running around the highway.

On one adventure, we found an actual tunnel that led out into an arroyo that was on one side of the highway. Then another tunnel that dumped out at the edge of the parking lot of the mall.

IT WILL RAIN

For people who don't know what an "arroyo" is, it's a very dangerous ditch, but it's concrete and really wide. The tunnel ran right underneath the freeway.

The thrill about crossing an arroyo was that at any second, at any time, water could begin flooding and rushing down the arroyo and into the tunnels. So if you were going to cross this way to get to the mall and risk your actual life, you had to be brave *and* stupid because if the water came, there would be no possible way to escape it. This is why before we began to make our way across, we would stand on the edge and think about it. That's not to say thinking helped. We never once decided *not* to cross the arroyo. We did it over and over, and in no time we were in Spencer's Gifts looking at their PG-rated sex products.

We didn't have mall money. Ever. So we did what normal ten-year-olds do. We begged for change all day long and made a shitload of money every time, Janelle, Jackie, and I.

Jackie didn't enjoy dangerous activities because she had morals and she didn't feel comfortable doing things our parents forbade us to do, as opposed to Janelle and I, who considered being told not to do something encouragement to do the thing immediately. Jackie was the worst liar in the history of lying. I loved her, I still love her, but she didn't have the rebel gene.

It was a competition to see whose line and whose acting performance succeeded. If it didn't work, you had to think of a better spiel. You'd have to really give it up to the strange adult if you wanted the change.

The line that never worked: "I lost my parents in a house fire and I need to eat at the food court." The line that worked most often: "I need bus money." By the way, that line still works. I can't say how many times I've given someone money for the bus. And when they say bus, they mean Bud. Whatever. I'm happy to help.

So we were doing our thing, making quarters hand over fist, mainly Janelle and I, while Jackie stood there with her hands over her face saying, "Oh my God. Oh my God."

I approached a lady, and in the most Oliver Twist kind of way, I said, "Ma'am? I can't find my mom and I need money for the bus to get home." Who knows why that worked, but she patted me on the head and handed me two quarters.

Ten-year-olds are notorious for not being all that bright, so I walked away and I was no more than two feet from the lady who gave me the quarters. I saw Janelle had dumped all our change on a washing machine in Sears. There was about thirty dollars in change on the washer as I flipped the two quarters on top of the pile and said, "Sucka!"

Janelle and I high-fived each other as Jackie inched her way behind a refrigerator in horror. I didn't even have the chance to turn around when the compassionate, kind woman who just had tears in her eyes when I told my story of sudden abandonment spun me around and pointed her finger in my face, "You are a disgusting little child. Give me my money."

I hear, "Oh my God." It sounds like it's coming from that refrigerator. Are you kidding with me lady? Even after I give you back your two quarters we will be chewing gum and riding metal horses outside for the next six hours.

Instead of just handing the lady two quarters, I pretended I was searching for the actual quarters she gave me because even at ten years old, I was hilarious. She grabbed two quarters off the pile and said, "You're a filthy

IT WILL RAIN

beggar!" and stomped away with her goofy-looking children.

There was a horse ride in front of Sears that had three metal horses on it. The three of us sat on the horses for hours putting our beggar money into the little slot. Did we feel bad? Not that much. We had pockets filled with gum, candy and money, and the horses went around and around. We would go around so many times eventually we would feel sick, but we never had the sense to get off. We'd just sit there hugging the metal bar with our eyes closed and our mouths wide open, drooling.

The day with the angry lady our consciences unexpectedly struck us. It also may have had something to do with the fact that my Uncle Cecil, Janelle's father, worked at Sears where we had done most of our begging and had been informed by his boss, via the angry lady, that his children were panhandling in the large appliance section.

We got tossed out of Sears by my Uncle Cecil. We hung our heads and very sadly walked to the arroyo tunnel knowing we had disappointed someone we loved as we blew bubbles with our pockets overflowing with money. Our pockets were so full of money and delicious candy we could hardly bend down to run through the tunnel.

Walking back through the neighborhoods, we came up with an idea that would enable us to repay our debt to society. We decided to give all our money to Mama Lia. She was poor. She needed money. But we knew Mama Lia wouldn't just accept the money because she was too filled with pride and gin. The three of us agreed on a plan, but we had to execute it quickly because we were in big trouble for begging at Uncle Cecil's place of employment.

We walked down the street and approached Mama Lia's house, but we came up the side of her house so she didn't see us and invite us in to talk about people we didn't know. Mama Lia had a concrete birdbath in her tiny front yard. The water swirled around and it even had a little waterfall for the birds to enjoy. We decided, because were ten, we would dump our giant pile of money into the birdbath. Mama Lia would wake up the next day and realize she was rich. So we dumped the change into the birdbath and we quickly walked away feeling like children of God before we could see the change go down the drain of the birdbath. Excuse me Heaven! It's us! Let us in!

The next day, we were walking down the street and we saw Mama Lia standing by her birdbath in a yellow dress with giant white daisies on it. Mama Lia was suddenly rich beyond her wildest dreams. But wait a minute. Mama Lia did not look happy standing there staring at her birdbath with her hands on her hips, shaking her head.

We walked up to her using our beggar acting skills and she was cursing, "Some dumb ass put change in my beautiful birdbath! It's clogged and broken." Jackie's skin began to blotch and she covered her mouth with her hand. We all tried to help and get the change out of the birdbath, but it was futile. From now on the birds would be dining elsewhere.

Aside from completely destroying her birdbath, I think us girls took a tiny piece of Mama Lia's loneliness away, even though we were in it to get a candy bar. But we learned something that day. We learned not to dump change in a birdbath and we discussed it the following weekend when we were begging for change in front of JCPenney.

Lawn Art

There were several forms of currency my mother used as I was growing up. One, of course, was cash. That was a form of payment we didn't use very often. There were food stamps, which were used once a week, and it was the most glorious day of the week.

I would always go with my mom to the store so I could sneak in a box of Ding Dongs. The cashier would scan the Ding Dongs as my mother stood in front of her holding her food stamps, and the cashier would shake her head. My mother has always been timid and quiet, and she would shrug in embarrassment.

The most anticipated payment method was Green Stamps. We got Green Stamps when we did our grocery shopping and the cashier would ask, "You collecting your Green stamps?" She asked this because some people didn't collect Green Stamps. They were cash people. Rich people.

As the cashier doled out the Green Stamps, I would smile because I knew we only needed 16,000 Green Stamps to get a brand new three-inch front yard garden gnome.

Figurines placed in the front yard always represented a perfectly put-together family, and the style of lawn art depended on the region where the family lived. People in Florida and senior citizens had bright pink pelicans in their grassy front yards while the homes in my area had a child size Jesus statue praying in a brick-arched display case.

I would watch my mom fill up book after book of Green Stamps, licking each one and placing the sticky stamp on the designated square. One after another until when she would speak, her lips would stick together and her tongue would make a popping sound.

Then she would count each book and look at the ceiling, counting in her head, assessing how many more books she would need to get a plastic punch bowl with six tiny matching cups with handles. Her finger in the air, drawing the line, carrying that number, and then looking at the pile of books in disappointment.

I was the only child of all six children that found the Green Stamp process thrilling. I would flip through the Green Stamp book and dream about all the interesting things we could get if we were rich. The morning of Green Stamp shopping, I would wake up and run to my parents' room pleading with my mother to quickly get ready to go to the store filled with worthless merchandise. If there was something you didn't want or need, it was in the Green Stamp store.

The payment exchange in the Green Stamp store was almost identical to the trade for tickets at Chuck E. Cheese's. At Chuck E. Cheese's, for six hundred tickets you can get a psychedelic pencil. The Green Stamp store used the same exchange rate. For 13,000 Green Stamps, you could get a three-ring binder.

My mother would look for things we needed while I ran around the store looking at toys and lawn art.

My mom was ready to check out. She was holding a shower curtain, a toilet plunger and a crochet tissue box cover. These three items were Mom's reward for collecting thousands of Green Stamps for five months. I had the tiny yard gnome in my hand pleading with her to spend part of her Green Stamps fortune on the gnome. She said, "Put it back. We don't need that." Need it? It's a luxury item, Mom.

If you didn't have enough Green Stamps, you could pay cash for the balance, so this was what my mother had planned. The cashier told Mom the cash balance as she was digging in her purse handing the lady one dollar at a time. A line began to form as Mom nervously searched for money. She was saying, "I had it. Right here," shaking her head.

This was common. My father would take the hidden money and not tell my mother and she would get someplace and have no money. My father bought alcohol with the money, so Mom was constantly hiding money from my dad.

The line was now longer and I could see my dream of the lawn gnome proudly sitting in our dirt-filled flower box in the front yard quickly slip away. Again. So I placed it on the gum rack at the check stand.

My mother was becoming irate, rifling through her purse, pulling things out and setting them on the counter, all the while angrily saying, "It was right here! Right here!" The people in line were rolling their eyes and shuffling their feet in annoyance. Mom finally went all the way over the edge and dumped her entire purse on the counter, screaming, "It's gone! It is gone!"

The cashier showed no mercy and dryly said, "Well. What do you want to do? Take off the plunger?"

Mom was furious, "I need the plunger."

The cashier said, "Shower curtain?"

Mom said, "Take off the tissue cover," as she jammed the contents of her purse back into her purse.

We got in the car and I nervously said, "The shower curtain was a great choice." Mom didn't say a word.

My mother and father took daily walks on the ditch bank that ran behind our house. Actually, every house we ever lived in had a ditch bank conveniently close for taking walks.

They had six children and when they headed out the screen door, one or five children would jump up to walk the ditch bank with them. My father was a fast walker, so my mother had to keep pace as we would trail behind or race past them, sticks and rocks in hand.

The ditch bank was quiet and peaceful. We would begin our journey, leaving chaos behind, traveling toward stillness that was only steps from our front door. The water running, the sound of the dirty water splashing against rocks or a tire someone had disposed of.

The ditch bank was positioned in a way that as we walked, we could see people's backyards. Then it would open up to a huge piece of land that, in the winter, was a blanket of snow, but in the fall, the trees surrounding the property looked like you had stepped into a beautiful painting. The leaves were yellow, orange, and red, and they fell in circles around the bottoms of the trees. Some areas of our walk had this view on both sides. Every time we rounded the curve in the ditch path this scene was waiting for us.

There were houses on the properties of these stretches of land and I would wonder what their lives were like. All they had to do was look out their window. It was like they were IN the painting.

During the walks on the ditch, we were an ordinary, typical family. Whatever insanity that had transpired the days or nights before disappeared from our heads. Our home was not in nonstop turmoil, but there was a daily feeling in the air that today might be the day our father wouldn't come home. My mother wouldn't say a word as the house fell silent and we would carry on as if everything was normal. Our father would walk in a few days later.

So getting to walk on the ditch bank with our mother and father symbolized that we were fine. Our life was fine and it was comforting to throw things in the ditch and look back and see our parents taking a walk like ordinary people.

There were obvious drawbacks to having an alcoholic father and a quiet mother, but there were things that my parents did that now, as an old lady, I can look back on and see as being quite extraordinary.

My parents never fought in front of us, which blows my mind because if my husband didn't come home even for one night, I would go bat shit nuts.

How did they do it? My mother never went ham on my father in front of us. We may have heard slightly raised voices behind their closed bedroom door, but they never went "full metal jacket" in the living room.

After a week of silently waiting for my father to come home, he would eventually come home and my mother and father would walk on the ditch bank. During those "dad-just-got-home" walks, we were not invited, but we all knew that by the time they returned, our lives would be back to normal. The following day, we would be invited on the walk and we were ordinary and typical again.

My husband and I will throw down anywhere. I can talk to my husband and one of my daughters in one breath, "Go fuck yourself. Do you want to go walk around Ross?" I know it's wrong, and I wish I would have taken my parents' discipline into my marriage, but I don't choose when to tell my husband to go fuck himself. He does.

My parents had much more good than bad. They did not spank us, although, there was about a week-long introduction to spanking because people had told them this was the way to go with kids—spank them. But because my parents were very calm, quiet people, the spankings were awkward and hilarious.

My mother would announce to one of the kids, "Okay. Did you put dirt in the neighbor's sun tea that was sitting on their front porch?"

Kid, "Yes."

Mom, "I'm going to spank you now."

Kid, "Okay."

Mom, "Come over here and lie butt-up on my lap."

Kid, with the other kids watching and laughing, "Okay." The kid lay on Mom's lap. It was all just very unnatural.

Mom, "Okay. I'm going to spank you now."

Kid laughing, "Okay." Mom would lift the belt and pop the kid on the butt.

Mom, "I'm sorry."

Kid laughing and talking with their face to the floor, "It's okay, Mom. I deserve it."

The audience of siblings was encouraging Mom, "You need to spank him harder. He did a terrible thing."

Mom, "Okay. One more and then I will be finished spanking you."

Kid, still laughing, with brothers and sisters laughing with tears rolling down our faces, "Okay Mom! Hurry! The blood is in my head!"

Mom would lift the belt and hit the kid with zero aggression and with an awkward swing. She would sort of turn her head like she couldn't even watch herself swing the belt. The belt barely hit the kid as he would roll off her lap in hysterics as the other kids were saying, "Did you learn your lesson? Mom. He should be spanked again."

We'd hear this conversation from behind their closed bedroom door:

Mom: "I'm just not comfortable with spanking the kids. I don't think I'm even doing it right."
Dad: "Are you spanking them hard enough?"
Mom: "What's hard enough? I mean, I don't want to hurt them."
Dad: "The idea of spanking is to hurt them. They should know they've been spanked."
Mom: "Well, if that's the point, I don't want any part of it. I'd rather raise savages."
Dad: "Well, I don't think they're savages." Dad looked out the back window. "Is Kevin rolling in the mud? He's covered in mud."

The spanking method lasted about one week. Then we went back to our father privately talking to us about our bad behavior and that lasted almost an hour. It was awful. I did take that example from my parents. I've never spanked my savages.

The walks on the ditch bank made my family ordinary. Living in a home where the ground is always moving, feeling ordinary is the best possible outcome, and it gave us wonderful memories of our childhood. It taught me that a walk in a quiet area can change the way my head and heart are feeling.

I would like me and my husband to start taking walks, but we live in the middle of Phoenix. We don't have the luxury of having a quiet ditch bank steps away from our home. If John and I took a walk we would have four people asking us for change and three people trying to sell us Meth.

I think this is how I learned to handle or not handle problems in my life. I learned that if there's nothing you can do to change it, just go on with your day. I do believe this is the best way to handle most situations. But I used this method for everything in my life including events that really haunted me, and that's why I couldn't get out of bed for eight months.

A healthy dose of fear is fine. I can say for sure that if my husband didn't come home from work—he knows, I was raised in a trailer—I would throw his shit on the cactus in the front yard. I know if I didn't come home, my clothes would be packed, outside, and he would roll back and forth over my iPad with his truck. It's healthy, normal fear, right? It's marriage. But to not say a single word? For the twenty years I lived with my parents. Not one, "Where have you been?" Never?

Five years ago, John and I were looking for a house to lease. We looked at several when we came across one really great house. As the owner showed us around, we walked in the backyard and sitting in a flower box was a garden gnome. It was partially covered by dirt and had been sitting in the hot Phoenix sun for so long the color had faded. But a gnome is a gnome. I immediately thought of the Green Stamp store and saw this faded gnome as a sign.

I'm finally like the normal people. Today, garden gnome. Tomorrow, brick-encased Jesus.

Thirty-Six

I published a book called *Everything I Never Wanted to Be* in 2010. I wrote about the following experience in that book. At the time I wrote about this, I purposely scanned over the top of my memory.

When I had to edit the book (which means going through the book hundreds of times to rewrite it, over and over), I would skip the page this story was written on. I wrote it, which was brave, but I was not brave enough to read it again.

I should have known by the reaction I was having that this day was an actual problem. One time when I walked by my office and saw that book on the table, I shoved it under a pile of paper just because of the three paragraphs detailing this day.

I'm telling the story again, not because the story in itself is so important, but the way I responded to this memory is important. I had no idea I had lived my entire life being a hostage to this memory. I didn't make the connection until I became depressed.

It's important to give proper attention to trauma. It's important, even if it happened thirty-six years ago, to resolve it and put it in a place in your head where it becomes manageable so you don't have to live as a hostage.

Ninety-nine percent of our sorrow we actually can walk away from. But there is that one percent, that one memory, that one day that we need to completely unravel from beginning to the end, so we can start living the life we were intended to live. You can't go under it, you can't go over it. The only way to redemption is to go through it. It's the most important lesson I have ever learned.

It's very difficult to tell a story you've been told not to tell. Of all the memories of the past fifty-three years, I can tell all those stories, but not that story. I can think about the terrible times or the beautiful times, but I can't think about *that* time. I can talk about anything, but I can't talk about *that* thing.

To deliberately write the story causes fear, because there are still so many people I love attached to the church or attached to other religious organizations and my words make them feel protective of their beliefs. They too want silence. They will sacrifice human beings for their distorted beliefs, not in God, but in religion. They will sacrifice their own to be a part of the community of people that all started with the best intentions. What began as their connection to God became a connection to the actual structure of the building, potluck dinners, kid church, kid's camping trips, and singing in the choir. Somewhere in all that, the lines are blurred. Right becomes wrong. The scriptures that once gave comfort became a tool to spiritually abuse in the name of Jesus. Pulling out bits and pieces to convey *their* beliefs, not God's. To defend *their* hate, not God's.

Without a doubt, most people who go to church once or twice a week are good, loving, spiritually connected people. They love this community of people and have complete trust in the people that lead them. Most priests are good, loving, and true representations of God's word.

But our faith is not tested until it's tested, and when we fail that test, we destroy people.

I have written about this event before in the most minimal way possible. I skimmed over the top and because of my strength as a human being, I've always believed this event did not affect me. Because I'm strong—strong like an ox.

I went that day to a previously arranged Saturday confession, a plan made by my parents and our parish priest. Asking for forgiveness in confession was the only way Jesus would forgive me for stealing a bag of hosts and savagely eating them behind the school next door to the church. I also ripped a sacred cloth by accident. Anything sacred rips easily.

I was sixteen years old.

When I got to the empty church, the priest told me it was too hot in the confessional and he would hear my confession in a back room. He systematically pulled a sheet across a string or line of some kind and the sheet separated him from me. His movements were so deliberate that looking back now, it is clear he had done this before. I sat on a gray chair on one side of the sheet and he sat on an identical gray metal chair on the other side.

I told him my lengthy list of sins and when I finished he said, "Is that all? What about the boyfriend?"

I didn't know what to say. I didn't know what he was asking. He said, "Are you having premarital sex?" I could see his outline through the sheet. I saw him stand, and it seemed like he was adjusting his clothing. He sat back down and began asking me questions—really vulgar, sexual questions.

After a few minutes of these questions, I was stunned when I realized he was masturbating. It was the most surreal feeling I've ever had. I thought, Is this real? Is this really happening?

Everything in the room changed and suddenly the air felt thick. His breathing was labored and erratic and while the questions were sexual and graphic, his voice was filled with anger and rage.

My eyes filled with tears and I didn't blink.

The only two people in the entire church were me and him.

The longer he spoke, the more disturbing the language was. He was irate and aggressive and violent. The only thing he said that wasn't sexual was that God was disappointed with me, but then he transitioned immediately back to the vile sexual rant. I was shaking; my teeth were chattering.

The walls were white, the door was white, and the doorknob was gold. For whatever reason, I was trying not to make a sound, crying without making any noise, silent and terrified. I opened my tear-filled eyes really wide and held my hands tightly over my mouth.

He went on and on as I stared at the blurry gold doorknob and my eyes filled with tears faster than I could allow them to drop. I knew if I could move fast enough, I could get to the door, open it, and get out.

As he spoke, for a moment I thought I was going to pass out. The whole room was moving and I closed my eyes and put my face in my hands. This feeling passed and I decided I had to make a run for it. I had to get out.

I waited about thirty seconds, jumped at the gold doorknob, got out the door and ran as fast as I could down the center aisle of the church, pushing the heavy wooden doors open and running through the parking lot.

The strong winds blew dirt across the parking lot and it covered me. I jumped into the car sobbing, locking the car door.

I got home and I was still hysterical. I went into a bedroom with my mom and dad and told them what happened. My father immediately did not believe me because, he said, I disliked the priest, which was true, but everyone disliked this priest. My dad said, "You ran out? That is so disrespectful." He was so angry.

I don't remember my mom saying anything, but the look on her face seemed like she *may* have believed me. She was looking at my father and sort of shaking her head quietly.

Then my father said, "You're going back and you're going to apologize to him." I cried and screamed, pleading with my father not to take me back to the church. He was furious and grabbed the car keys and told me and my mother to get in the car.

This was thirty-six years ago. In my father's defense, back then, to believe a priest would do such a thing was unheard of. It just didn't happen. Ever.

We drove back to the rectory of the church. I looked at the priest, he looked back at me, and I apologized. I was told not to bring it up, ever. I walked out the door of the rectory as my parents followed behind.

This was the first time in my life I felt crazy. I was filled with confusion because I knew it happened, yet, the adults told me it didn't. Maybe it didn't happen and it was me. The priest had told me while he was masturbating that God was disappointed with me. Maybe it was true that God was disappointed in me and I didn't see or hear what I saw and heard?

In my sixteen-year-old mind, forgetting it ever happened was the best course to take. Don't think about it. Don't talk about it. It never happened.

I got in the car and didn't say a word and neither did my parents. We drove home in complete silence. I never cried a single tear until the day I took that nap thirty-six years later.

About fifteen years after that day in the church, my mother called me very upset. My father had already passed away. She opened the morning paper and saw the same priest was being accused of sexually assaulting many, many children and young people.

It's the day that left me permanently, mentally and spiritually derailed from the person I could have and should have been. I couldn't talk about it, think about it or write about it for thirty-six years. I kept the secret. I spent thirty-six years shaking this memory out of my head.

I have felt alone and invisible my entire life—completely and utterly alone. But now I know I absolutely had to go through this depression to come face-to-face with this day, to find peace and hope and regain my faith in God. And regain faith in myself.

Before I became depressed, this day would enter my mind about once a month. I was always able to shake it away quickly. But during my months in bed, the memory of this day was a permanent slideshow in my head. Several times a day, unprompted, I would remember the sheet or the doorknob or the wind.

When my depression got really serious and scary, I thought, I'm feeling so many things, but what is the number one feeling? If I could sum it up in a word, what would it be? Invisible.

There's a point of feeling invisible when you feel less than all other people. Then there's a lower point of feeling invisible when you feel you actually aren't a human being at all. You're not here. You're not real. Everything you see and hear is either happening or not happening and you can't figure out which is the truth. The things you see with

IT WILL RAIN

your own eyes cause confusion. The things you hear with your own ears cause confusion. So you live every day not having any idea what is real.

I think this comes from emotional trauma. Adults telling me an event didn't happen when it did happen caused a break in reality in my mind. It's equivalent to having brain damage.

Then I thought about the other unbearable, distinct feelings. Humiliated. Trapped. I didn't come to these things in a short time. It took months to narrow them down and then it took months to mentally walk through all of these things and realize why I felt the way I did.

I wanted this to be a fast fix, but it wasn't. I had to process that day from the beginning to the end, over and over, until I began to feel desensitized to it. I had to allow myself to feel whatever I was feeling, let it out, then go through it again and again. No more ignoring it or fearing the thought of it or minimizing it. I was easily able to minimize it because I thought about the other young people and the fact that they were physically sexually assaulted. So because I wasn't physically attacked, it was easy for me to say it was not a big deal. I was able to feel compassion for the other people, but I couldn't find compassion for myself.

I had nonstop panic attacks. I thought about it and I didn't stop until I could think about it without tears or panic. No matter how painful, I stuck with it; I sat in it; I rolled in it. And when the fear was gone, I could confidently say to myself, it happened. And it wasn't my fault. And I am a person worthy of love and life. My anxiety disappeared.

It took many months, rage, tears, and sadness to get to the clear reason for the way I felt my entire life. And when I did figure it out, it was shocking.

I spent thirty-six years thinking I was strong because when this event entered my head I was able to shake it away. Pretend it didn't happen. Don't talk about it. Don't think about it. I felt that admitting this event had a negative effect on me and was a reflection of my weakness as a person. I've had an amazing life and then I have that one day. One day. Who would have thought one day could have such an enormous impact on my life. For thirty-six years, I have had an extreme phobia of being trapped, being in any situation that I can't get out of—airplanes, the freeway, drive-thru windows, walking too far into the mall where I am unable to still see the door that leads to the exit, elevators—I could go on forever. If I feel trapped, I hyperventilate. The exact feeling of staring at that doorknob surfaces in any situation I feel I can't get out of. Now I know my reason for this particular phobia came directly from that event. Not knowing that all these years is mind-blowing to me.

I can't imagine a higher authority figure for a Catholic girl than a priest. Over the last thirty-six years, if a person in any position of authority took advantage of anyone, it didn't even need to be me, I became uncontrollably enraged and made every effort to plot their demise. I would aggressively find a way to expose their misuse of power and not in an "I'm-going-to-fight-for-the-underdog!" sort of way. For example, watching or hearing about an authority figure abusing their power would make me feel like I was going to pass out. That kind of rage. I've never passed up the opportunity to verbally unleash on people who do this, no matter the negative outcome, directly related to my experience from so many years ago, and it's caused me to burn many a bridge and piss off countless authority figures. Well, I pissed off authority figures that were abusing their authority. And the mother fuckers deserved it. I'm still working on myself.

IT WILL RAIN

Having to apologize to the priest made me feel humiliated. Since then, I have been in a constant state of humiliation. How I look, how I dress, how I talk, everything about me makes me feel shame. That's just how I feel as I go on with my day. It's always there and it never goes away. This is one of the primary feelings that caused me to lie in bed for eight months. I woke up every day feeling humiliated and hurt. Every day. I actually said to myself, I don't understand why I feel this strong feeling of humiliation. No one has caused me to feel this way. I don't get it. Until I got it.

After apologizing to the priest, I felt invisible. I felt I didn't matter as much as other people. So since that day if I'm overlooked in the slightest way, I will tear people to pieces. Again, not a normal way to respond to people. And ninety-nine percent of the time, my view of being overlooked was completely unintentional.

I felt he picked me because I was worthless. I felt my father didn't believe me because I was worthless. It was my fault. This is what I believed. Every blaring character defect in my life was directly related to that one day. One experience.

The day I took a handful of my mom's Klonopin was my third trip to the psychiatric hospital. I have lived a life of drugs, alcohol, anxiety, panic attacks, depression, and rage.

So when I walked away, did I walk away? I did walk away. But I walked away a completely different person than the person I was supposed to become. I walked away humiliated, shamed, and invisible.

Sometimes parents just like me make mistakes that cause horrific harm. That was never my intention with my children or my father's intention with me, but that was the outcome. I know for sure my father never knew the damage that was caused. I know without a doubt that if he was alive and I asked him about that day, he would do everything and anything to fix that mistake. I am positive about that. I don't believe my father would ever disregard my account of what happened knowing I would live with this for the rest of my life. I know my father loved me. I know for sure he always loved me. He made a huge mistake. Huge.

When something traumatic happens in your life and you walk away and try to erase it from your mind, what it does is fill you up—with anger, fear, sadness, and confusion. I had gotten a clear message in my life about this day: to leave it alone. Don't dig up mud from thirty-six years ago. Let it go. I agree, completely. The problem is that it doesn't work. I've tried to remove that day from my head for thirty-six years.

I think people also feel that if I'm willing to talk about the greatest pain and secret in my life, they are reminded of their pain and their secrets and they don't want to talk about it.

I've tried to forget it, let it go, walk away. I've tried praying. I've tried convincing myself it didn't really happen. I've tried ignoring the memory when it pops in my head. I've tried telling myself it wasn't a big deal. I've tried pretending that it didn't have a horrible, train wreck of an effect on my life. I've tried abusing drugs and alcohol to have just one minute of peace in my heart. And all these things lead me to the same conclusion: It happened. But I must keep the secret because of the fear. Don't say a word. Keeping the memory of this day a secret, it is the equivalent of treading water in the middle of the ocean.

Secrets are like being bullied, and the key is standing up to the bully. This took thirty-six years to figure it out. A long, long road.

Another thing that continued to surface during my depression was the fact that I have made mistakes as a mother. Big mistakes. The girls have forgiven me, but I can't seem to forgive myself. Again, like magic, that day floats to the top of my mind because it's an obvious question. Is it possible that I really didn't forgive my father and that's why I can't forgive myself for the mistakes I've made as a parent? If I truly, with my entire heart, forgive my father, will that help me to forgive myself? Are these two intense, heartbreaking feelings actually connected to one another?

So I knew, because my father is not alive, I had to accept the fact that I'm not going to get any answers. I had to forgive my father in order to forgive myself. It didn't happen overnight, but after a few months I felt I really, really did forgive him.

Then I spent time trying to forgive myself. And eventually I did. Again, it didn't happen overnight. After an ocean of tears and heartbreak for my girls, I found forgiveness for myself. What an amazing feeling. It felt like a heavy weight dropped off my shoulders.

I think this is what happens. We are born. God has a plan, or path if you will, for our entire life. That path never changes. God's plan for us never changes. But when horrible things happen we can be completely knocked off our path. Sometimes we are knocked off just a few steps. Other times, with more traumatic events, we are knocked off our path a million miles away.

When people talk about their soul and their concept of what the soul is, I find it annoying and stupid. I also understand that it's confusing to read about the "God, soul, and spirit" deal from a person who says the F-word fifty-six times a day. I'm a mixed bag.

I have realized my soul is the only authentic part of me. It's the real me. It doesn't change with hurt or hard times.

It remains the same—true, authentic. My soul is the person God brought to the earth. It's the only part of me that can't be altered. When I'm on the path God wants me to be on, that's when I am most connected to my soul, therefore, most connected to my real self.

The first step was discovering I was off my path. Then, it was walking that million miles back to the original plan. Step by step. I realized this horrible event derailed me a million miles away from being the person God brought me here to be. So what I did was imagine what I thought God had planned for me and did that. I decided to become someone I would be proud to be—kind, loving, understanding, and compassionate. Forgive my father. Forgive myself.

I haven't done this perfectly, but now I'm aware of my words and actions. There are still days I am not even close to my path. Some days I'm rolling around in a shit ditch in the wilderness. But I try to take a step, and then another step, back to my perfect, safe place. Back to my soul, back to God.

When this day entered my mind, I would shake my head like an Etch A Sketch. I thought if I actually thought about it, or processed it, terrible things would happen. What if I went crazy? What if it pushed me over the brink? But then I realized that *because* of not addressing this day, I actually *was* crazy. I was already over the brink. So the only thing that could happen would be good. That enormous emotional load would lift and I could get my life back.

The other thing I believe is that if I am negative, violent or cause pain to the people around me that will put me back in the shit ditch. No human being is born bad. So even the most flawed person can move in the direction of their path, step by step, and become the person that God brought to the planet.

IT WILL RAIN

What redeems me and all people is that God knows when we are pushed off the plan he set for us. Because while some may live life without the misfortune of being mentally or spiritually beaten away from God's plan, others may not, and God knows this.

So if you are a stable, successful businessperson with a pretty house and beautiful family and someone else is a heroin addict living behind a garbage dumpster, God views both of you as being equal—the same—because God has the backstory. See you in heaven!

Now I look back and wonder, What was I supposed to be doing the past thirty-six years? I don't think I was meant to be intoxicated or high or depressed. What would I do if someone removed that day and made my heart whole, and gave me back thirty-six years? Wow! I could be anything? I could do anything?

I would have been kinder. I would have loved more and laughed more. I would have been a better mom, wife, sister and friend. It would have been different.

The most unforgiving thing about living a life that wasn't planned for me is time. That time spent not being my authentic self, I can't get back. I can't get it back. Thirty-six years living a life that was not mine. Time. I'm like a bag of ice sitting in the sun.

I wish I had more time. That doesn't mean I can't still become the person God planned. But I have to do it with a broken-down body and a head full of memories, good and bad.

The most brilliant spiritual leaders have written about this process of self-discovery: Eckhart Tolle, Marianne Williamson, Deepak Chopra. I only know this because my smart friends give me inspirational books and they always say, "This book will. Change. Your. Life."

I don't want to confess that I'm not intelligent enough to comprehend the book, so I try to read it and always feel more confused. I get distracted. For example, Eckhart Tolle sounds like this: "The past is not real. The future is not real. The only thing that's real is right this second. How many chucks can a woodchuck chuck if a woodchuck could chuck wood?"

Marianne Williamson: "Our deepest fear is not that we are inadequate. Our deepest fear is that we are powerful beyond measure. This land is your land. This land is my land…"

John also gets these books as gifts. I swear to god, I can open one of John's books and it actually cracks because it's never been opened.

The problem I've always had was trying to figure out what they were talking about. I would have to go back and finish high school, go to college and then become a doctor just to understand the book.

You know who desperately needs to understand these books? People like me. People that are sitting on their rent-to-own furniture eating Cheez Whiz off a pencil. Dumb down, gurus.

Travel in Poverty

Dominique, nique, nique,
S'en allait tout simplement
Routier pauvre et chantant.
En tous chemins, en tous lieux,
Il ne parle que du bon Dieu,
Il ne parle que du bon Dieu.

My two older brothers, Mark and David, spent much of their time trying to work me up. I only weighed about nine pounds, but if I got frustrated enough, I would unleash on anyone. My brothers thought this was hilarious and they gave me the nickname "piranha."

They never bothered with my sister Lisa because if you walked toward her she would drop to the ground and curl up in the fetal position crying. Not me. I was always on stand-down just waiting for mayhem to ensue. They would laugh and tease me while I tried to ignore them.

They would put their hands up to their mouths like they were talking on a loudspeaker announcing some big event, "And here comes piranha! She looks angry! She's small, but she's a maniac! Show us what you've got piranha!" Most of the time, it didn't work, but every now and again, I would pounce on one of them like a cat. Or like a violent fish.

As part of my Catholic confirmation (which, by the way, is an actual Catholic event complete with school, Bible teachings, and a crispy itchy dress), I was asked to assist one of the nuns in the bookstore of the church and when I say bookstore, I mean bookshelf. I had never met this nun before and I honestly can't remember her name, so let's call her "Sister Sledge."

Sister Sledge didn't know me. She didn't know I sinned from the time I woke up to the time I went to sleep. And they weren't even accidental sins. I knew I was sinning all day long and I just continued to do it.

Of course, on that day I was trying not to sin because I was working in very close quarters with a nun—a full-blown, fully dressed-out nun. I think I was about twelve. I do recall being so young, when Sister Sledge said she was going to go to the restroom, I remember being shocked that nuns go to the restroom. At that age, I thought nuns' bodies were exactly like a Barbie—smooth with no parts.

I remember the exact moment I was tidying up the bookstore/bookshelf and Sister Sledge began to inquire about my future. The truth is, I never thought about my future past lunch. I knew I would probably continue with the extreme sinning, but past that, I had no plans. This was the moment I knew Sister Sledge had no idea who she was talking to. She said, "Have you ever thought about becoming a nun?" I turned away quickly and stared at the books thinking, Oh my God, did she just say that?

As I looked at the books, Sister Sledge was looking at me waiting for an answer. I mean, even my parents knew that for me to stop sinning even for a few hours a day was unusual. So what an honor that someone believed I could entirely stop sinning. Without skipping a beat I said, "Of course I've thought about becoming a nun. Doesn't every young girl?"

We spent the rest of the afternoon with Sister Sledge explaining to me what it took to become a nun. The main thing was that I had to stop sinning.

I was walking home on the ditch bank and thinking that, while some people might find this laughable, if I stop sinning now, yes, I could actually become a nun.

Aside from the information Sister Sledge gave me that afternoon, the only other thing I knew about nuns I learned while watching the Singing Nun. The Singing Nun was a really pretty, guitar-playing nun. She was sort of a hippie nun and she sang the *Dominique* nun song:

Dominic, nic, nic
Goes along very simply
Traveling in poverty and singing.
On every road, in every place,
He just talks about the Lord,
He just talks about the Lord.

As I walked down the ditch bank this song played in my head, although, I only knew the first line, "Dominique, nique, nique." I imagined every step I took was a step away from habitual sinning and a step toward being a seasoned nun. By the time I arrived home my family had no idea I was a changed person/child.

The first thing I had to do was get a handle on the incessant sinning. The way I assessed sin when I was twelve is the same way I assess sin now at the age of fifty-three. If something is really great and amazing and hilarious?—Sin. If something is boring and stupid?—Not sin.

I said to myself that if I just take one moment at a time, I could become pure. Every time I was invited to sin, I could sing in my head, "Dominique, nique, nique ...

Dominique, nique, nique ... Just travel in poverty ... Talk about the Lord."

I was challenged immediately when I heard a bang on my bedroom door. It was my brother Mark, "We're taking the bus to the mall. Mom said you can't stay home alone so you have to go with us."

I asked him why he, my other brother and their friends were going to the mall when they didn't have any money. He mentioned something about a "five finger discount." If you're a sinner, you know what this means, and although I didn't say it, in my mind I thought, Watch your fucking mouth. I'm a nun.

Of course I knew the snowball of sinning was going to start rolling down the hill because my brothers were also straight-up sinners, sinning the second we left the house. Smoking cigarettes on the way to the bus stop. Cursing. Punching each other. Spitting.

We got on the bus and I sat in front of my brother and his friend and stared out the window. Dominique, nique, nique. Trying to not even open my mouth because I know if I did, a sin would come out.

My brother was sitting behind me tapping me on the head, tapping me on the ear, he and his friend laughing and laughing. The thing I had learned in the first two hours of being a nun is that the world is going to challenge you. Your brothers are going to challenge you. You have to be strong. I heard my brother with his hand in a circle up to his mouth sounding like a speaker, "Nobody knew 'piranha' rides the bus! I hope nobody gets bitten!"

You could always talk yourself into saying that what you're doing is not a sin, especially when you're twelve. My job, and clearly the only reason they took me with them, was to talk to the cashier while the boys shoplifted candy. I wasn't the one shoplifting, my brothers were.

That's not to say that I hadn't shoplifted a hundred times before this day, but I was a different person than I was three hours ago.

You would think that because I distracted the cashier, the thieves would have shared their candy with me. We would both be wrong.

We walked through the mall while the boys had circles of different colors around their mouths from their giant jawbreakers, red, blue, yellow. "Hey Dina. The red jaw breaker taste like cinnamon. Too bad I'm not going to give you one." Dominique, nique, nique. Travel in poverty.

We walked through a department store because it was a shortcut to get to the bus stop. There was an above-ground pool set up in the department store filled with water. The bottom of the pool was lined with pennies, nickels, dimes and quarters.

The boys clearly had not sinned enough for one day and began to discuss that if someone jumped into the pool and swam around on the bottom, they could grab a bunch of change. I was standing several feet away from the boys because I felt there should be distance between good and evil.

Suddenly, I was under the freezing water. It only took me half a second to jump up out of the water and forget I was a nun. "Mother fuckers! You fucking mother fuckers!" By the time I surfaced, I saw the boys running out of the glass doors of the store howling with laughter.

I climbed out of the pool bringing about five gallons of water with me and also ran out the door. There were four or five of us and we were running through the parking lot while a couple of employees from the department store were screaming at us as they stood out on the sidewalk in front of the store.

We ran and ran, me slower than the boys, my clothing heavy because it was soaking wet and my shoes were filled with water. Then these idiots had the nerve to act like I failed because I didn't take the time to get any change.

I was furious. I didn't even sit next to them on the bus, although, I could hear their speaker voice a few rows back, "Piranha! Can we get an interview? I see you just came from out of the water!"

When the bus dropped us off, I was even more aggravated because I was walking down a dirt road soaking wet, so it turned into mud all the way up to my knees. Both my brothers, David and Mark, gave me a jawbreaker. I think it was an apology.

I always found my brothers to be extremely entertaining even when I was the target. It was sort of an honor to be their constant source of entertainment.

The old "sinning me" would've jumped into the pool and scooped up an assload of change. I tried not to sin for more than six hours and I was exhausted.

The absolute center of our little world was the ditch. Every single thing we did in our day involved the ditch. Meeting a friend, walking down the ditch, throwing things in the ditch, trying to pull things out of the ditch, and of course—the highlight—pushing someone in the ditch.

Let me explain the ditch for those of you who have lived a charmed life. The water in the ditch was muddy and stinky; it reeked. Some areas of the ditch rushed with water while other areas stood still with a layer of toxic green film. The smelliest part of the ditch was overrun by bugs, mosquitoes, lizards, snakes, spiders—anything that could bite you lived in or by the ditch. For whatever reason, this never bothered us.

If you went to bed at night and you hadn't been bitten at least twice, your day had been wasted. If these things happened to my grandsons today, I would call an ambulance and they would go straight to the emergency room.

Back then, I could run into my mother's room in a panic and tell her, "Mom. Kevin's face is swollen like a balloon and he says he's blind. He got bit by something."

My mom would be sitting on her bed, wetting the tip of a thread in her mouth, then rolling the thread in her fingers, shutting one eye as she held up the needle, focused, still, pushing the thread through the tiny hole, clearly satisfied with this accomplishment. Then without even glancing at me says, "Tell him to put some Mentholatum on it."

Spider bites, dog bites, strep throat, broken heart, Mentholatum was the only cure aside from giving it to God, which had proven to work better than the Mentholatum.

We were small children, but we could walk around the dirt roads for ten hours a day. My best friends, Jeanette and Patricia, and I would meet halfway on the ditch. It was easily five miles to their house, but we did it about ten times a week. There were secret places in various locations along the ditch. Hiding places. Who are we hiding from? Vampires. My brothers. The ditch witch.

"La Llorona," a.k.a., the ditch witch, was a scary story many parents told their children to keep them from playing by the ditch. The story of La Llorona is that a mother with a couple of small children fell in love with a man who did not want children. So the woman drowned the children making the man not want her, so she drowned herself.

The story is that this dead woman walks the ditch banks crying for her children and looking for other children to drown. They say she only comes out at night, so during the day we would spend hours looking for her footprints. It never dawned on us that not once did a child ever turn up missing.

Every home I grew up in was located next to a ditch. I would lie in bed at night really still and quiet trying to listen for the crying of the ditch witch. Finally, one night, I heard the ditch witch crying. I jumped up and ran to my parents' room and led them by the hand back to my room where, oddly, the crying had stopped. This went on for a couple of weeks. I would hear the crying, run to my parents' room, and the crying would stop.

I lay in my bed, staring at the ceiling and again, "La Llorona" crying. This time I didn't move until she actually tapped on my window. I jumped up and ran to my parents' room just as my brothers came through the back door of the trailer laughing, Mark scraping his shin on the wooden steps. But they both continued laughing hysterically, tears rolling down their faces and blood dripping down Mark's leg.

I swear to God it looked like my dad was trying not to laugh. When I lay back down and realized the ditch witch was actually my brothers, I was relieved and I fell asleep as Mentholatum wafted throughout the trailer.

I never did become a nun and I'm still sinning regularly. I thought maybe when I got older I could be a nun, but I never did have the desire to stop sinning. Every single thing I wanted to do would be classified as a sin. I struggled to think of activities that would be fun and hilarious that were not a sin. I still do.

My husband John is the biggest sinner I have ever met. He has the nerve to sin and then lie about the sin, which is another sin. I'm not exaggerating when I tell you if I say the F-word twenty times a day, John says the F-word at least seventy-five times a day. Although in our house we don't call it sinning, we call it enjoying our life.

IT WILL RAIN

John is wrong all the time. Most of our marital problems are caused by John because of his propensity for sinning and wrongdoing and because he has zero desire for spiritual growth. Spiritually, he's seven and that's okay because financially, I'm five. So, it's an even trade. At least I think it is. Travel in poverty. Talk about the lord.

Deepak

I think in an average lifetime, every person comes to the place where they have to fight for their life. The reasons vary—divorce, financial destruction, death of a loved one, or even depression.

There are seasons in our life when we have to self-talk every day: "I have to fight for my life. I have to get up and over this. I have to fight."

Some people fight for their lives more often than others, but all of us will get to that line in the sand. Change has to happen, and you have to make the needed changes, but by the time you get to that line, you are flat on your back, no faith, no hope, your body aches, your heart aches. It's difficult to physically move. To be in a position where you have to fight for your life sucks. It really sucks. But I know we all come to that day at some point in a lifetime.

So to fight for your life feels huge and impossible. It turns out that all the advice people give you ends up being the solution. You have to move, get clothing on, get out of the house, and all of these things make you feel better. Activity gives you the tiny bit of fuel you need to begin a full-blown fight for your life. Take a step, take another step, until you are able to do something as simple as walking down the street.

What happened to me in this depression was more than just losing my "stuff." Getting a divorce or losing your house, car, or losing everything, we've done that several times. It was like that scene from *The Grinch Who Stole Christmas* as the Grinch walked out only leaving exposed wires hanging from the walls. We've done that three or four times.

I lost my inside stuff—like hope. I lost my faith, my mind, and my heart. I found that I needed my inside stuff to appreciate my outside stuff. The inside stuff is the foundation for all change, action, and happiness. Without it, I was going into battle with no ammunition.

I had come to the conclusion that in order for me to dig my way out of this depression, I was going to have to fight really hard. My only comfort was cigarettes, and I smoked one after another.

I waited many months for it to magically go away and it just didn't happen. I had to physically start moving, which sounded easy, but it wasn't.

One day, my husband John came into my room and said we should go to dinner, get out of the house. He was sure I would roll over in my Corona T-shirt and say no as I had done a hundred times before, but this time—I'm not sure why—I said yes. I immediately regretted it.

Word got out around the house that I was getting out of bed. They were all staring at me, sort of shocked, mumbling to each other, whispering, "She said she's getting out of bed. She just said she would go to dinner. I have no idea what's going on. She's sitting on the edge of the bed. She looks like Bob Marley."

Going to dinner sounds easy, but it took every single ounce of physical strength I had. Every step exhausted me. My daughter Carly came into my room and said, "Mom. Get in the shower. It's just dinner."

IT WILL RAIN

I didn't want to do it, but I showered and put on clothes, rolling my eyes and complaining the entire time. I walked out the front door and had to shield my eyes from the sun like the kid from the movie *Powder*.

Carly went with us, almost pushing me out the door, and we went to dinner like normal people. There was a moment during dinner when I looked around the restaurant and studied the people talking, smiling, and laughing. I heard glasses and plates clinking together, the sounds you hear in a restaurant.

I couldn't imagine any of these people having their lives pulled out from under them because of something as trivial as depression. I was out, in public, wearing clothes.

John, Carly and I talked and laughed and ate, and for a moment, I was happy. I did have short moments of anxiety, but they passed quickly.

After dinner we were driving home and Carly said, "Mom. I want to take you somewhere. Just say yes." This already didn't sound good. The last time she said she was taking me somewhere, I ended up in the mental ward. I told her I had already done something. I wanted to go home and get back in bed without being hassled. Carly ignored me and continued to stare, waiting, as if I answered wrong. After a couple of moments of complete silence, I reluctantly agreed, with the worst possible attitude. Carly had been clean and sober for many years and she was going to pull me out of the hole with or without my consent.

It seemed like there had been several occasions where I had to do the whole "fighting-for-my-life" ordeal. I really didn't know if I had the strength to initiate a fight for my life, much less execute one. The truth was if I was crossing the street and I saw a big bus coming at me, I probably wouldn't rush.

I was on the fence about dying, which would have been horrible, but also about living, which would have also been horrible.

There weren't very many appealing things about life when you laid it out. Most of life, at least in my house, was full-blown noise. I had never been the twelfth caller for free concert tickets. I'd never had anyone give me the wrong change in my favor. You know, the perks. I'd never gotten a free soap sample in the mail. I'd never had a celebrity sighting (other than the comics I worked with that are now famous and have no clue who I am. That scenario was actually a perk that was given to me and then taken back as gasoline was poured on my self-esteem).

So I was stuck in the middle. I didn't want to be here, but I didn't want to *not* be here. There are people in the world that live every day in the most depressing, hopeless environment. They live in desperate poverty or have debilitating health problems. What is their heart saying to them that my heart wasn't saying to me?

They had the resilience of the human spirit and I saw it all around me every single day. I didn't have any of the problems above. What made people fight so hard for their lives when I had a complete disregard for mine?

Carly had pulled the truck into the desert wilderness. We walked to an entrance where a sign said "hiking trail." I was pale. It hurt to walk. As I walked and complained, Carly said, "Every negative thing you say takes away from the beauty." So I was silent, breathing really hard because the only thing I was intensely committed to in this life was chain-smoking.

The trail was crowded with people. Carly said, "See all these people? You think they are climbing this mountain for their physical health, but they are actually climbing it to feed their spirits. To feed their souls. You need to do activities that feed your soul. Like hike. Or paint a picture. Or cook a really weird Indian dish. That's how you will get back to normal. All we have in this life is our body, mind, spirit, and soul. If you feed those things, everything else works out." Thank you Deepak.

I was completely out of breath, "So sort of do an *'Eat, Pray, Love...'* But do it here in Phoenix because I can't afford to go to Italy? Or Tibet? Or to a doctor?"

Carly, "Yes."

Carly walked in front of me not breathing hard at all, almost skipping. I thought it would be hilarious as people passed to yell to Carly, "You said we were going to the Olive Garden!" The people laughed. Carly didn't.

We climbed and we climbed. There were various points of the hike where I looked out at the city and wondered if a helicopter would be able to get in there to airlift me out. Finally, it seemed like about twelve hours later that we came around the corner and arrived at the top of the mountain.

I sat on a giant rock, out of breath, and looked out at the entire city that was visible from every direction. There were butterflies everywhere flying around, so beautiful.

I couldn't believe I did it. I know to normal people it doesn't seem like a big deal. But to me at that moment, it was huge.

I sat on the rock and thought, All this is out here. These are the things I can't see from my bedroom. Life is always happening with me or without me. I sat quietly and looked out and it was so beautiful and calming.

After my breathing returned to normal, we began our descent back down the mountain. I commented on how proud of myself I was because of the difficulty of the trail. Carly said she was proud of me also. Then she explained that this mountain was the easiest hike in the whole state of Arizona. The entire way down I discussed the difficulty of the trail.

Then I said something. Feelings. Carly was saying something about being "in the now" and why the "caged bird sings" and I blurted out, "What am I going to do when dad dies of a heart attack?"

This created a screaming fight about how negative I am. My automatic response to being told I'm saying negative things is to say more negative things. I explained to Carly that that's the reality I live in every single day and what about mom and what about Jen and April and what about my grandsons and what about my hair... You get it.

She walked away and said that she was not speaking to me until I stopped saying horrible things. I followed behind like a four-year-old breathing really hard. We got in the truck and I said, "There was a high level of difficulty."

She drove away and got to the stop sign and said, "Everyone has stuff, mom."

I had to say yes when everything inside me said no. I enjoyed the hike. There is a whole world out there and I don't have to have any money to go get it.

So was that the end of my depression? Nope. I got back in bed. I woke up the next morning and I was so sore I couldn't move. I lay in my bed staring at the ceiling thinking about my amazing dinner and how I had made it to the top of the mountain. As I began to fall asleep I thought, My stuff is worse than your stuff.

The days after my hike with Carly, I spent in bed. I didn't understand why. I felt so great when I arrived at the top of the mountain; I believed I was cured. I believed I left my depression lying on top of the rock I sat on because I walked down feeling weightless and free. So imagine my horror when I woke up and *it* was still there.

IT WILL RAIN

The dread of the day. The black sky, again, struggling. The crackle of thunder.

So I realized this was not going to be as easy, or as funny, as I had planned. It would be work. John bought me workout clothes the day after my hike and they sat on the floor in the bag with the tags still on them. Every time I looked at that bag I felt irritated.

One evening Carly said, "What do you think when I say, 'Guided Meditation class?'" I thought what any typical person thinks, Kill me. I had ZERO desire and it actually sounded like torture. Carly said, "Just say yes."

I did not want to do this, but I said, "Whatever. Fine." She told me to wear something comfortable, so I pulled the workout clothes out of the bag. Of course l looked like a complete idiot because every workout meditator would know my workout clothes were the clothes people buy when they had no intention of working out or meditating. It seems like I've seen some people on TV working out in my outfit. It's amateur night at the Guided Meditation class.

We went to a Buddhist Temple. Carly had been there before and she knew the drill. Of course, the avenues for comedy were everywhere and it began with the woman who greeted us and actually whispered, "Hello. Welcome. Please take your shoes off."

We took our shoes off and were led to the meditation room where other people sat, also shoeless. It was very quiet and no one spoke. I did what everyone else did.

The room began to fill up. The altar in front of us was beautiful, and I knew each thing had meaning, but I didn't know what the meaning was. There were five or six statues of Buddha, all in spectacular colored robes of red, orange, and yellow—an eruption of color and candles—sitting right in front of us.

This is where the memory of Julia Roberts in *Eat, Pray, Love* sitting with the all-knowing Buddha veers off course. As we all sat in silence, I noticed a door open next to the altar and I held my breath.

Something was happening. I did what everyone else did. They stood and put their hands together as if in prayer. Then, a tall, white librarian-looking lady walked out in socks up to the altar and sat in front of it on a big pillow. A WHITE WOMAN. I thought, A tall, white woman? Are you kidding with me? Where's one of those guys? I hope I'm not sounding racist right here, but the little bald guy, the guy that sort of looks like Buddha? He would be wrapped in a colorful Buddha wrap. No. Tall, white woman. I got robbed at meditation.

I quickly decided to play along because this woman must've known something or she would have been sitting on one of these folding metal chairs instead of that fluffy pillow. So I just did what she said. I focused on relaxing, being calm, still, and quiet.

We did that for ten minutes and to be honest, it seemed like ten seconds. It was nice for someone to tell you exactly how to relax. For lack of a more accurate word, it's relaxing.

Then she began the spiritual teaching. As she spoke, sort of in a whisper, she told us about all the things we are supposed to do every day. Then she told us what we are not supposed to do. Of the things we are supposed to do, I did none of them. Of the things we are NOT supposed to do, I did all of those things every day, all day long.

The topic was "delusions" and apparently I had all of them. I had delusions about other people, but I had more delusions about myself. She said these delusions are fiction and are only there to cause me pain and unhappiness.

IT WILL RAIN

I had convinced myself I had seen what life had to offer. It was a ton of tears and sweat. I often said when I looked down the road at the rest of my life, I couldn't see anything. There was nothing waiting for me. This is what I believed.

So this lady was saying that I had to retrain my mind and, of course, this was not new information. It's just, how would I make that happen?

When I left the Buddhist Temple, I felt a little bit cleansed and hopeful. The tall white lady did give me so much to think about and for a moment, I actually thought that she was speaking directly to me. That, of course, is another delusion.

The things we tell ourselves. The things we tell other people. The idea that we have been appointed to knock people down a notch or two as if that's our job. One thing I know for sure is that people who run around "telling it like it is" or "telling another person's truth" are weak people. Not strong.

Strong people have a filter and have the strength not to hurt people even if they think it is deserved. People have *the right* to say or do whatever hurtful things they think we deserve, but according to white Buddha, we have the right to reject their opinion.

The negative things we tell ourselves, we are also allowed to reject those thoughts. But with Buddhism or any spiritual practice, it's something you have to practice and work at every day.

These things gave me a stepping stone to the next thing, which will be another stepping stone to enlightenment. Getting out of bed, I stepped on a stone. Hiking up the mountain, I stepped on another stone. Guided meditation, another stone. At some point, I hope to have stepped on enough stones that I make it to the other side—where people go to the movies and laugh and cry and just live life—and that's all I want, to live a life. I want my insides back.

Loco Anna

Caring for my mother in my home for eight years took an enormous toll on me in every way—spiritually, mentally, and physically. Her Parkinson's disease and dementia had progressed to the level where she was in an unending state of confusion. She was incapable of remembering even hours before.

The frail, trembling, elderly woman was disintegrating in front of my eyes. She couldn't comprehend simple directions, and her voice was so small and fragile I struggled to understand her explanation of the hallucinations she was positive were happening. I was completely and utterly drained.

Before she became really sick, I was able to get her take on difficult situations I usually placed myself in. She always had the perfect answer. She was kind, compassionate, and understanding. She was that person in my life that was always in my corner and believed I was always innocent. It's good to have at least one person like that in your life.

It's possible that caring for my mother in my home for so long contributed to my depression. Feeling backed into a corner, I tried to avoid upsetting my mother by having her continue living in a home where her caregiver (me) was on the brink of suicide. She loved her room at my house.

I felt that my mother's life had been so chaotic and heartbreaking, I didn't want to do something that would make her feel more hurt. The thing I needed to do for me and my life was to have my mother live someplace where she could get the care I couldn't give her.

I felt completely responsible for my mom and her feelings and I didn't want her to feel unwanted or unloved, so I ignored my feelings of being suffocated with responsibility. Every aspect of my mother's life sat directly on my shoulders and it was breaking me in half.

At some point, the pain in my neck became completely debilitating, figuratively and literally. I hadn't been able to do anything I was normally able to do like type, drive for more than half an hour, or pick up my grandson, Matt.

At night I began waking up at about three o'clock in the morning with crushing pain in my right leg, neck, and shoulders. At about five, I would succumb to the pain and get up because the only thing that helped to alleviate it was movement.

I was diagnosed with an illness called fibromyalgia; osteoarthritis in my knees, back, hip, and neck; and degenerative disc disease. All of this was because of the horrible physical jobs I worked my entire life, then moving mom in and lifting her for another eight years. I would walk into my mom's room, see her lying on the floor, and my entire body would catch on fire at the sight of her.

You think it would be easy to find a bell. Mom had a bell that she would ring if she needed something, but she lost it. I needed to be able to hear the bell from the other side of the house, so it needed to be loud, not cute.

I never found a bell, but I did find a whistle. A rape whistle. It looked like an ordinary whistle. So mom would blow the rape whistle and I would take her lemonade.

IT WILL RAIN

We would hear a scream. Two or three of us would begin to run like cattle down the hallway to Mom's room. But on the way to her room, the scream was always followed by a crash into a wall, door, or the shower doors in her bathroom. We would slam into one another running down the hall in panic. Then walk in and find her lying on the floor, flat on her back.

She had a variety of reasons for why the falls would happen. "I just went over." "Someone pushed me." Once she said, "This is a bunch of bullshit."

Mom fell about ten times a day, so the idea of putting her in a nursing home entered my mind every single day. Every now and again, I would attempt the nursing home conversation and mom would become very upset.

We would pick her up and check her for injuries. According to her, she was perfectly fine and was never hurt. Mom wouldn't be honest if she was injured because she believed the doctors at the hospital actually had the power to put her into a nursing home. So if I asked Mom if she was okay, one hundred percent of the time she would say she was fine.

My mom got smaller as she aged, but it was still picking up an adult person lying flat on their back from off the floor. When my husband or daughters were home I could have them help me, but if they weren't home, the only way to get her off the floor was to pick her up myself, hence my destroyed neck, shoulders, back, and legs.

I would do my best to check her over, give her back the rape whistle, and remind her for the millionth time to blow the whistle if she needed to go anywhere. Or blow it if she was actually being raped.

One day, after falling off the toilet twice, falling into her shower and knocking both her shower doors off the rails, I noticed she was limping. I checked her over, but something about the way she was acting was more off than normal. I asked her over and over, "Mom, it seems to me that you're hurt."

She of course said, "I'm fine."

I decided to take her to the emergency room, and every time I did this, it infuriated her. I explained that I needed a doctor to check her out and do some x-rays to be sure that she was okay. We had done this about ten times.

We would go to the emergency room, they would do all the tests and x-rays, and then they would tell me everything was fine. They always said her "vitals" were like a twenty-year-old's. I would nod in agreement. Well, not nod because I couldn't move my head, but I would blink in Morse code because my eyelids were the only part of my body that didn't hurt.

So her insides were like a twenty-year-old. Her outsides were like she was two hundred and sixty. She's a German car. Then they would say, "She should be in a nursing home." Every. Time.

On this day, I took her to the emergency room as Mom mumbled and complained the entire way. I figured we would be home by noon. When we had to go to any kind of medical facility, Mom always wanted to rehearse answers to the questions they would ask when they were trying to determine her mental state.

So on the drive over, Mom mumbled, "What is today?" I told her it was Tuesday. I asked who the president was. She said, "Osama."

I told her she was close, but so far away, "It's Obama."

We went into the hospital room and they gave her a gown. I undressed her and put the gown on. Elderly people bruise easily and I was used to seeing Mom's bruised body from the constant falling. She had a bruise on her hip where I suspected there was an actual injury, a bruise on her lower back and also bruises on both of her knees.

IT WILL RAIN

The nurses and doctors were asking her questions which she did answer, but no one could understand her except for me because I speak Parkinson's. They asked her what day it was and she looked at me because she had already forgotten. I said, "It rhymes with Useday." She said she was not sure.

They asked who the president was and she said, "Osama." They asked if she knew where she was and she said, "Arizona." She looked over at me and I gave her a thumbs up because what am I supposed to do? Tell her she blew it?

I don't have the thought process that normal people have. I don't take time to think about a certain situation, weigh the pros and cons, talk it over with people, and then come to a final decision. I burn the candle all the way down until the flame burns my fingers.

I looked at my mom lying in the hospital bed with the bruises, nonstop mumbling, and the disturbed, crazed facial expressions of a person with dementia. She was shaking and twitching and my heart completely broke in half because I knew right at that second my mom was not coming back home with me.

I immediately felt the crackle of thunder hitting my stomach. I couldn't breathe. I knew without a doubt I could not care for my mother another minute. My husband and daughters and I did the absolute best we could for as long as we could, not leaving one second to spare for me to scream for help. I couldn't pick her up one more time. I physically couldn't do it. Because I swear to God if I could have, I would have. I had to be able to walk or crawl around the world for the next twenty years if God gives me that.

I was sitting on a chair in her hospital room watching her and felt completely paralyzed knowing it was already done. It should have been done years before this day, but I didn't have the heart to do it.

Not bringing Mom back home that day was not my intention, but when I looked at her bruised body in the bright lights of the emergency room, it disturbed me. I could not allow my mother to live this way. She deserved so much more.

Mom fell asleep and I walked out into the hallway with my neck, shoulders, and legs on fire. I felt dizzy. I pulled Mom's doctor aside in the hallway and I told him, "I am not a doctor or nurse and my mother needs people with the medical knowledge and equipment I don't have." He said he agreed that she should be in a nursing home. I explained to him in order for Medicare to finance a nursing home, my mom would need to stay in the hospital for three days. I reminded him of her head-to-toe bruising and told him she was clearly not safe in my home. I also told him this was not what mom wanted and it was not what I wanted, but it was painfully clear she needed actual medical care.

This doctor looked at me like I was the biggest asshole in the world confirming my feeling that I am the biggest asshole in the world. He said she definitely should be in a skilled nursing facility, but he did not know if he could accommodate me trying to, in his exact words, "work the system" in order to get Mom the basic medical care she needed.

The doctor didn't understand that I couldn't afford to self-pay for a skilled nursing facility, although, there was no doubt in anyone's mind that was what she needed. He acted as if I had some kind of nerve trying to get my mother medical attention. I was enraged at his attitude and I felt all the blood in my body rush to my head. I was livid because this mother fucker probably never spent one day picking his mother up off the floor, much less eight years.

IT WILL RAIN

I was trying desperately not to cry. I know this happens to people all the time, but it never happened to me. My hands began to shake from the rage. I swear my throat felt like it had completely closed shut. I tried to get a breath and I couldn't, I started wheezing, I was completely panicking, trying to scream, "I can't breathe! Help me!" I grabbed the doctor's arm and I turned to my daughter Carly and said, "I can't breathe! I can't breathe!!"

I could hear myself gasping for air. I sat down on a chair with Carly telling me to calm down and after a while, I began to breathe normally. The doctor told me I was under a lot of stress and this was a panic attack. He told me he would see what he could do about getting Mom admitted.

That evening they transferred Mom to a room in the hospital. Every single doctor that saw her said she needed to go into a skilled nursing facility. A physical therapist worked with her for about an hour and said she was not a candidate for physical therapy and needed to go into a skilled nursing facility. Every single nurse that cared for my mother asked me how I was able to do this even with the help of my husband and daughters. They said she needed care twenty-four hours a day and in order to move her out of her bed, it required two people to do it safely.

I grappled with the right words to explain to my mother why she was not coming home with me and I knew I was in for a mumbling shitstorm.

The hospital neurologist said she was not safe in my home and she definitely needed to be in a skilled nursing facility. He suggested I talk to her about it with him in the room so that he could verify that the conversation happened, for her safety, so that's what I did. The neurologist stood there quietly as I explained to Mom she not only needed better care, but that she deserved it. The neurologist agreed.

I explained that I had a family and two grandsons and all sorts of activity in my life; I couldn't do this anymore with my health issues, but there were places she could go where she could get the medical attention she deserved. I told her she couldn't spend the rest of her life lying on the floor waiting for me to come home from the grocery store.

Mom wasn't happy, but it was time for her to get medical treatment and time for me to salvage my parts because I still had a long road in front of me.

On the afternoon of Mom's fourth night in the hospital, her chirpy caseworker walked in and said, "We are just having a heck of a time trying to find a nursing home that will accept your mother." I asked her why and she told me Medicare would not cover a skilled nursing facility because Mom did not meet the three-day inpatient hospital stay requirement.

Complete confusion. I said, "But she's been in the hospital for four days!"

She said, "Yes, but she's listed as 'outpatient.' "

I said, "But she has not left the hospital for four days. I know this because I've been sleeping on the couch in her hospital room for four days."

She actually looked at me with a little smile and said, "Yep. It's a loophole. It's a horrible system. There's nothing we can do about it."

I was baffled beyond belief and I said, "But that's wrong. That's not right."

My throat was again about to close shut. She looked at me and said, "It is wrong. You're going to have to go ahead and take your mom home and in the next month or so, hopefully, her caseworker will be able to find her a proper facility."

I said, "But the neurologist said she was not safe in my home. So Medicare is telling me to take her home anyway?

And they know she's not safe? And they don't care? Really?"

I knew for sure that if I took Mom home with me she would be there another year and one of us would be leaving by ambulance. I told the caseworker, "No. I can't take her to my home where she is not safe because Medicare is trying to save money. I won't do it. Every doctor she's seen has said she needed a skilled nursing facility and she is not safe without twenty-four-hour-a-day care. She has been here for four days. Tell Medicare I will not take her home."

Now this was the second time in four days someone looked at me like I was the world's biggest asshole.

There was no turning back the clock. My mind was solid. I stomped out of the hospital in a rage, crying. I was hyperventilating and smoking and walking around the parking lot talking to myself, sobbing.

I was so angry they were expecting me to swallow this loophole and be polite because we were poor people and this is how poor people are treated. Just be polite like the other poor people. I'm not even polite when I'm being polite.

About an hour later, the caseworker walked in with a doctor. This doctor looked like one of the Backstreet Boys. He was the same age as my daughters.

The doctor explained to me, in almost the exact words the caseworker used, if they were unable to find my mom is suitable facility, I would have to take her home with me. He said the problem was that she was classified as outpatient so it took away approximately eighty percent of her benefits provided by Medicare.

Then I went back and forth with the doctor about the fact that my mother hadn't left for four days. He said, "Yeah. It's a horrible system." I was furious. He smiled his fifty-thousand-dollar smile and it took every single ounce of restraint I had not to punch him square in his fucking sexy throat.

About an hour and a miracle later, the caseworker walked in and said she was approved at a facility and that they would be there soon to collect her. I went to the nursing home and it was absolutely amazing. I stayed for a few hours, tucked mom in, and drove home for the first time in four days.

Mom had been there for five days. "We're going to have to transfer your mom somewhere else as soon as possible. Medicare is refusing payment because her stay in the hospital was outpatient." Then I was handed a bill for more than three thousand dollars that they said needed to be paid immediately.

I was given the name of another facility and after seeing it, I felt it would be perfect for Mom. I explained to the admissions lady, in detail, the way Medicare was refusing treatment and she said she would do what she could to get Mom transferred.

I went back to the facility that was kicking mom out, and on the way in the door, I was again handed the three thousand dollar bill and asked for a credit card. I was out of my mind with rage.

I drove to the hospital where my mother had been an "outpatient" for four days. A caseworker took me back to his cubicle and said, "You signed this piece of paper. It clearly states we classify some patients as outpatients."

I was fucking livid. I said to him, "Do you think for one second I would sign anything *knowing* that my mother's medical benefits might be taken from her? Are you out of your mind? And the fact that you have a piece of paper for people to sign when they come into the hospital in total fucking distress—a paper that removes their right to medical care—tells me that you come across people like me all the time or you wouldn't have paperwork to cover your ass."

He took me back to the administrative offices where I could file a complaint. I spoke with a woman who was nervously scribbling my complaint down on a message pad as I sobbed and screamed. I told her that we were not giving anyone a "message." Whomever she was planning on giving this message to, I needed to speak to them now.

She walked away probably desperately scanning her mind to figure out who she was going to pass me off to as she was saying to herself, "Horrible system."

It seemed like seconds later, the vice president of the hospital walked through the door—a tall, elegant, beautiful woman who looked exactly like Sharon Stone. It didn't even seem like she was walking, but more like she was gliding or floating toward me with the *Touched by an Angel* glow outlining her physical form. For the fifty-third time I explained the problem with the word "outpatient."

She said, "It is a broken system."

I asked who implemented the system because it seemed to me that every person I spoke to thought the system did not work, except for possibly the person who created the system, and not one single person could figure out who that guy was, the "system maker." No one would admit to being that person.

She repeated that the system was broken and it made no sense, but she also had to follow the guidelines. The guidelines of the guy who created the system. That no one understands. That everyone thinks is stupid. That is causing damage to elderly poor people.

She was growing tired of me like most wealthy entitled people do. She said she would speak to one of the doctors that Mom saw while she was in the hospital and ask them to change her status from "outpatient" to "inpatient."

As she walked me to the door, I could smell her Chanel perfume and wondered what it was like to be awesome. She said, "I will do what I can." And I am thinking, *When she says she will do what she can, what she means is she will go to lunch at P.F. Chang's with the Backstreet Boy.* "We are not allowed to change a patient's status from outpatient to inpatient after they have been released because that is classified as Medicare fraud." Medicare fraud? Fraud is saying a patient is outpatient when they were inpatient. That's fraud.

Every now and again we come across people or multi-billion-dollar corporations that are corrupt. I don't think my mom will ever know that I really did try to fight for her. My mom didn't have any idea all of this was going on.

I drove back to the facility that was ten minutes away from setting mom on the sidewalk. I knew my mom was either going to be transferred to the other location or I had to take her back home. I had run out of options.

On my way in the door, a miracle happened. I saw the facility caseworker and she told me that Mom was about to be transferred by ambulance to the other facility I liked. I went to my mom's room and told her that we were moving her to a better facility. Yes, it was a lie, or Medicare fraud.

By good luck we happened to arrive at the new place just in time for lunch. Two nurses escorted us through the hallway to the dining room and, as they walked, one said to the other, "Let's sit her next to Loco Anna."

They pushed Mom's wheelchair into the dining room to a table and there she sat, Loco Anna. She was very tiny and very old. It was Halloween, so she was wearing a wig that had psychedelic bright colors of fake hair—green, blue, and orange. My mom looked at her and then looked at me because she didn't know it was Halloween.

IT WILL RAIN

I tried to tell Mom that this place would be okay and it was just going to take a little bit of time for her to get used to it. Then Loco Anna said, "I'll tell you one thing about this place, they have the best soup in the entire world, and trust me, I've eaten soup everywhere."

I said, "Really? Well that's good to know."

Then Loco Anna said, "See this onion soup? It's delicious. Yesterday, we had cream of potato. They make all their cream soups out of real, pure cream. I bet you didn't know that a lot of places use a powder? Not here. Pure cream. And here's the thing. We are allowed to order soup anytime we want, day or night. I could call a nurse at three in the morning and order some soup. If I felt like it, I could eat half of this onion soup and I could say, 'You know what, I changed my mind. Now I want some cream of potato soup.' They let us get away with anything here." You don't get the name Loco Anna by eating only one kind of soup.

"We have to move your mom. Arizona health insurance is refusing payment." Are you kidding with me? It had been more than twenty-five days I had been searching for a facility to care for my mom without the three-day inpatient hospital stay. I was too exhausted to say the F-word. Another miracle! Five days later, she got final approval by her Arizona insurance to stay where she was. None of the other facilities would be responsible for her because she was much too sick and she couldn't walk or get to the bathroom or do anything by herself.

One person told me she should be in the hospital. I laughed and said, "You are hilarious."

Mom was in the nursing home for a little over a year. She hated it there. I visited almost every day and she would tell me that the Russians had bought the facility and she didn't sleep because they had parties all night long. She said, "You know how Russians are."

    I made the mistake of hooking up her phone and taping my phone number on it so she called me about twenty times a day. It was always a phone call in complete panic, "Dina. The place is closed. I am here alone and there are chains on the front door." I would say I would check it out and she would add, "Bring some scissors to cut the chains to get in." Or, "Dina. They just brought in my suitcase and told me to get out because the Russians didn't pay the electric bill." Or, "Dina. They only allow us to eat Russian food."

    I say, "What's Russian food?"

    Mom says, "It's ice. They only eat ice."

    I knew the way insurance companies worked long before my experience with my mother. I know this for sure: Insurance companies don't give one shit about your health. They don't give a shit if your brain hemorrhages and you curl up in a ball and die in the middle of a kiddie carnival. They don't care about you. Period. They don't care if your child is sick. They don't care if your elderly parent is sick. They simply do not care if you are dead tomorrow. You could choke on a Peep on Easter and collapse in front of your children during an Easter egg hunt. You could be run over by a trolley at Disneyland that rips your legs off in front of your entire family, Snow White, and all the Dwarves, and you will not get medical treatment because of the "Disneyland loophole." They have a loophole in the event you are stabbed and end up with an actual loophole that needs to be stitched up. It's the "no loophole" loophole. A nun could be violently attacked by a yak at a petting zoo while she is holding conjoined twins that are ripped apart by a goat. They will only approve treatment for the goat. They. Don't. Care. Insurance companies don't care if you're white, black,

Hispanic, they don't care about clowns or teachers or Mother Theresa or Gandhi or Elvis. They will let you die so they can save fifty dollars. They are murderers. They are thieves. They smell bad. They're stupid. They're fat. They have terrible hygiene. And we are making them rich.

Two Medicare CEOs walk into a bar. Fuck them.

Five Minutes

I have a ninth grade education and those nine years, in terms of learning, is questionable. If it were not for spellcheck and a great editor, I would not have the opportunity to write and publish a book. I can't do math. I don't know a single thing about history or politics. Nine out of ten questions you ask me, I will not know the answer to. I have never known one answer to a *Jeopardy* question and I am not smarter than a fifth grader. Of the four things I know for sure, this is one of them: In my life I have tried countless times to get inpatient drug and alcohol treatment either for myself or for a family member. I believe most people think that all you need to do is ask for help and you can get help. It's not remotely close to being true. I know more people that have attempted to get help and failed than people who don't want help.

There is a physical and emotional stage in addiction when a person needs to be removed from their environment, for a time, to have a chance at staying clean and sober. They need inpatient medical treatment.

It's a common practice in America, the country I love, but a country with its faults, to deliberately and systematically cut funding for substance abuse and mental health treatment. These programs and services are the first to be financially cut because we are still of the opinion that addiction and mental illnesses are a moral failing and not a medical condition.

Many years ago there was a moment; it lasted about five minutes, but I can still remember that five minutes. I had been sober from alcohol addiction for about one month for the first time in twenty years. Very early one morning, I walked outside onto my patio, sat down and looked at the street that was in my view. There were no traffic or sounds as the businesses were not open yet and the rest of my neighborhood slept.

I sat in complete silence and heard something crackling in the distance. It was a leaf blowing gently down my quiet residential street. I watched it make its way, moving, then stopping, according to the demands of the blowing breeze. The leaf slowly tumbled down the concrete and I was mesmerized by it because it seemed like all the movement in the entire world had stopped except for this leaf.

That five minutes was the first time in my entire life I felt real peace. Complete stillness. I had never, ever been calm enough in my own skin to notice something as simple as a leaf blowing down the street.

It was the first time in my life that I felt I was okay. My insides weren't trembling. My skin wasn't crawling. It was the first time I saw the world in a comforting, calming way.

I cried, because I had never felt peace before this moment. I wasn't crying because I was moved by a leaf. I cried because I had no idea that this is how some people feel all the time. This is normal to some people. They take it for granted, and it is the most beautiful thing they possess—faith, confidence, fearlessness—the knowing that everything will be all right. They have hope. But they can't treasure that hope the way a person who has lived without hope can.

Of course later that day, the realities of life, traffic, bills, broken cars, and crying babies brought the chaos and noise back with a vengeance. But I referred back to that leaf blowing down the road as evidence that I do possess the ability to feel safe and calm. When people told me, "You're a good person," I never understood. After those five minutes, for the first time ever, I understood—I *am* a good person.

It was five minutes that opened a world of possibility, that I could actually fit in, I was good enough. For five minutes, even I could be accepted and equal to other people. For five minutes, I could take all my flaws, memories, and all the problems I had encountered and say, for the first time ever, it's okay. Everything will be okay.

I can still clearly remember those five minutes. Of course, after that I had many experiences with feeling calm and quiet, but that first time was such a stark difference to what I had felt my entire life. It was powerful. The voice in my head was new and encouraging and hopeful.

I hear stories about how someone has a loved one that is addicted to drugs or alcohol and that they went to treatment and it didn't work. Some stories are about people going to treatment six or seven times and it never did work.

There is a moment for every single person that is free from a certain chemical for a few weeks, where they experience these five minutes. For people that are addicted to any substance, it's safe to say they have never felt peace their entire lives. So when many people go into recovery or treatment, five minutes of serenity is very powerful. It's a feeling you will remember forever. It's a feeling that either becomes a way of life, which is what we all dream of, or it becomes the thing you spend your life chasing.

Once a person has those five minutes, they never forget. Where it used to be easy to forget your responsibilities, now you've experienced those five minutes and you have a constant reminder that you are capable of being the person God brought you here to be. Where you once spent your entire life with the devil on one shoulder, now you have an angel on the other shoulder reminding you, you are worth saving. You have good to combat the bad because of those five minutes.

And that is what the money for substance abuse treatment provides. Five minutes. Without experiencing them, there is little hope that an addicted person will ever recover. Because they only have one voice, and that voice is telling them there's no hope, they don't deserve to be happy, they are not good enough.

Those five minutes are the highest high. Some will stay clean and some won't. But the memory of the five minutes will become the high they will chase even when it looks like they have no hope.

People in powerful places will continue to do the same thing that we have done for the past one hundred years and it has never once worked. It has never worked, but we continue to do it. We pay for the perpetual rotating door to emergency rooms, to court, to jail, to prison, and then back to the emergency room. It goes around and around and it has never worked. It. Never. Will. Work.

If we continue to refuse to give addicted people a chance, to give them even five minutes of feeling hope, they can't get better. If we don't give people that five minutes of hope, change and peace is not possible.

If you want to change the world, give people those five minutes. It's worth every dime.

If I Could Turn Back Time

A friend passed away and my heart broke watching the immediate family plan a funeral while their hearts were so broken. It got me wondering about what will happen when I die. Who will do all of these things?

When you plan a funeral there is so much to do in a very short amount of time. So I'd like to make it easy for my family and plan it for you right now.

I would like to be cremated. I do not want, I don't care how much money I have, to spend $10,000 on a cushion box. I want someone to go to Ross Dress for Less and go to the housewares area and come up with something that could double as an "urn." Something fun and classy. Some of the items in Ross are questionable, so don't put my ashes in a pig cookie jar with a pig nose as the handle at the top of the jar. Have some taste.

After you "ash me," I want to be buried. Period! I don't want the girls to be walking around the house having a great laugh about something and then walk around the corner to see me sitting on a knick-knack shelf next to little Las Vegas shot glasses in a pig cookie jar.

The ashes of a deceased loved one do not create a beautiful, peaceful feeling. I don't care what other people claim. When I decorate my house, one of the main rules is: no dead people.

People say that you can have your ashes sprinkled in some really special location. If I could have my ashes sprinkled anywhere it would be a really glamorous, expensive place that I could never afford to visit, much less stay. So I would like to have my ashes spread about the lobby of the Betty Ford Clinic. And be generous. Make sure that every group meeting room has me in a plant in a corner, so I can at least get help from beyond.

I want great music and I want it playing when people are walking in the place, so they don't sit there jittery and uncomfortable. Pink, Cat Stevens, James Taylor, Beth Hart and don't forget Michael Jackson's "Man in the Mirror." And crank it up.

If, by chance, by the date of my demise John and I have won the lottery or are swimming in money, there is one thing I never did in my life that I would like to implement at the departure ceremony. I would like my ashes sitting on a giant half-moon that will be dramatically lowered from the ceiling while the song "If I Could Turn Back Time" by Cher blasts through the grieving people. I had planned on doing this on *The View*, but I was never on *The View*. As it is being lowered, the mourning people will gasp upon discovering the enormous half-moon is covered in glitter and completely bedazzled.

Now. During the service they do a thing called a "tribute." That's where someone walks up, fighting back tears, and talks about how blessed the world was because I was here. I have taken the time to write my own tribute so no one has to say weird things about how I lit up the room. A sobbing, destroyed family member will read this:

If someone is reading this, well (long dramatic pause), I am no longer here. I'm not thrilled to be in this position, but it is what it is. Jennifer, April,

IT WILL RAIN

Carly and my new son Michael, I love you guys. Know that you don't have to be unhappy. Know that there is an entirely happy way to live out there waiting for you. Go get it.

John, you are the love of my life. Till death did us part.

To those people I hurt, well, sorry. For all the people I don't like and who don't like me, nothing's changed. You were a douchebag while I was alive and you remain a douchebag in my death. I will take my complete hate and nausea at the sight of you to my grave. Don't eat anything at my reception, mother fucker. Being that it's obvious I am getting to heaven first because you are sitting there grinning and I am in this pig cookie jar, just know that every time you slip on some ice, there is someone in heaven laughing their ass off.

That said, this is no time for anger. The most important thing is that the people who love me not wallow in your sadness for a long period of time. A few tears are fine, but don't overdo. Except my husband John—I want you to cry forever. If you find love down the road, I will consider it a complete betrayal. Get used to being alone and sad, and know that if you are with another woman, I am watching you. Yes. It's going to be very creepy.

My husband, my children, my grandchildren, just do the best you can, every day. I've had a great life. I spent most of my life laughing, so I've been lucky. You guys are my whole heart.

The End.

Exit, sobbing, unless you feel like falling to your knees because of sadness and then someone could walk up and help you. I saw that on TV and hoped someone would do that at my funeral. I really want someone to grab my urn and begin screaming as they collapse to the floor. But that could go wrong in a hurry. So if it feels forced, just sob and then walk back to your seat.

After the funeral itself, I think at the reception there should be a "merch" table set up. For people not in the business (rolling my eyes), a merch table is an area where entertainers sell things to make extra money for narcotics, cocaine, and whores.

On that table should be my first book, *Everything I Never Wanted to Be*, and this book.

The other day, when I was coming out of a store, I saw a small child wearing a T-shirt. It had a photo of the Lord Jesus Christ (our personal savior) and right under Jesus was a photo of a man throwing a gang sign. Then, of course, the whole "RIP" and death date. I'd like that. I like the idea of a child wearing a shirt that reminds them of their deceased family member all day long. Have my daughter, April, fold them according to size and put them on the merch table because April is the only one who will do it right. Make sure there are children's sizes!

The money that is made from the merchandise should go back in the bank so that John does not have to carry the financial burden for the cost of the half-moon, glitter, bedazzles, and glue.

So there you have it. It's all taken care of. I don't foresee my loved ones having to implement this plan in the near future. But when they need it, it's here. We could actually start bedazzling the half-moon now and put it in storage.

Mr. Bojangles

In all the chaos and instability, the sound of my father playing his guitar would bring immediate calm. As children, we would hear him in his room begin to play and we would run from all areas of the house.

We would sit in a semi-circle and listen with pride because he was our father, and he was a rock star in the eyes of a six-year-old. He could bring the house crashing in around us with his illness, and hours later, put it back together by singing a song. It never added up that our worry and fear could be brought on by this guitar-playing man, singing with his "James Taylor" voice and strumming the guitar with such ease. The clouds always parted and everything was now okay.

His closer was always "Mr. Bojangles," so the feeling of hearing him sing this song was mixed. Even at the age of five you knew the free concert was almost over. But we watched and listened because it didn't matter that we had heard our father sing this song a million times; every time was a perfect.

No person can be summed up with one word, even an alcoholic or drug addict. The one true thing about my father is that he was an alcoholic. But if you put all the good and all the bad about my father in a big bowl, the good would outweigh the bad by a longshot. If I had a huge problem, my father was the one to talk to.

My mother was not a screamer, but about once a year she would begin to scream, and no one knew what she was going to say. It was as if she saved up all her anger from the past year and then it all flooded out of her mouth like boiling lava. The words were never harsh or sharp because my mother didn't have that in her, even if she was trying, but she did have the volume.

Because she only screamed once a year, when she did, everyone in the house froze where they were at, trying to listen through the walls to figure out what made the volcano erupt, peeking 'round the corner as she was furiously sobbing, slamming things on counters, slamming doors, and screaming about everything that upset her over the past year.

I remember like it was yesterday the night I told my father I was pregnant. I was seventeen years old. I volunteered to go with my father someplace, I don't remember where, but I did this so I could tell him the news that would not make anyone happy and it was guaranteed to cause my mother, the volcano, to erupt.

We were sitting in the family van parked in front of our house upon returning from wherever we went. I looked at him after I told him my troubles and he was silent for what seemed like forever. He looked down, then looked up staring through the windshield, then looked back down, not saying one single word for a long, long time.

I was dying because the silence was so loud. I mumbled something about how maybe I could marry the guy. My father, without hesitation, looked directly at me and said, "Do not add another mistake on top of the first mistake. Do not get married or even think about getting married."

Then we sat—more silence. The silence felt like it lasted six days. Then my father looked at me and said,

"Okay. We will do the best we can. It will be okay." We got out of the van and as we walked into the house, he said, "It will be okay."

I sat at the kitchen table and he told my mom her seventeen-year-old daughter was pregnant. Lava covered my feet. My father stood their agreeing with her, saying, "I understand," every few minutes. Mom went on and on to exhaustion, screaming and crying. Then what seemed like seven hours later, she fizzled out. I was head-to-toe in lava. As she calmed down, my father asked her, "Are you done with her?" which started her on another rant.

"Oh, I'm done all right! I'm done! I'm done! I'm finished! Get her out of my sight!"

My father looked at me and said, "Go to your room." I tiptoed out of the kitchen. My mother was over it by the following day.

A year or so after that conversation with my father, my little blue-eyed baby was in the front row, listening to my father sing and play "Mr. Bojangles" with undivided attention. Then other grandchildren came into the world, all just waiting for their grandfather to pick up his guitar.

I watched both of my small daughters watch my father, their eyes transfixed on his voice and the rhythm of his hands hitting the strings, their eyes darting back and forth from his voice to his hands. Then seeing the familiar disappointment we also had as children when he set the guitar in a corner.

Now the grandchildren would wait, like we waited, to hear the first strum of the strings, never, ever tiring of my father's gift of bringing us out of the darkness and into the light.

At my father's funeral, the last song we played was "Mr. Bojangles." All the people who loved my father, family and friends, we all smiled when the song began. We all celebrated his life and the legacy he left us; the legacy of kindness and the beauty in small things, like singing a song when the world is crashing in around you. How the simple things heal most wounds. How a man playing the guitar can take away all your troubles, even the troubles he caused.

My father was a writer, although, he was never published. I think about him often as I walk the path of being a writer. I thought of him when I was standing outside smoking right before I was to read part of my book at an event for the Chicago Writers Conference. I wondered what my father would think of this. Of all of the people in the entire world, I wish my father was here to see me publish a book. He has always been the only person I was ever trying to impress.

I know five guitar chords. My grandsons hear me play one stroke of the strings and come immediately from wherever they're at. Moses stares and smiles. Matt runs around the house saying, "Let's play the guitar, Grandma!"

So the person I am most mad at, I am most like. And I must say I am thankful for the things my father passed down to me. I could have done without him passing down the alcoholism, but the other things, I'm so, so lucky. You have no idea how many songs you can play only knowing five chords. Hundreds.

Dear Dr. Phil

I watch Dr. Phil every day. I'm on his side until he gets a hold of parents that have addicted children. Then I want to come through the TV and go ham.

There are rules and guidelines for people with loved ones who have an addiction. It's in all the books doctors read in college. But unless you are a doctor who has a child with an addiction, you cannot understand, you cannot get it. You can tell someone about the rules from the book you read, but the rules never have the heart of the parent in mind. Ever.

Dr. Phil goes ape-shit on these parents as they sit there, pale, dizzy; they haven't slept in seven years. He lays out the rules from the book and tells them they are out of their minds. And that's really the thing isn't it? Yes. The parents *are* out of their minds, so how could they make a clear, confident choice or decision?

That is not to say the rules aren't good ones. They are. They are exactly what you should do. So why don't parents follow these rules?

For these parents, their child is the light of their life. They love their child just as much as Dr. Phil loves his. But their kids are killing themselves right in front of them. Every day. Every day, countless parents all over the world wake up and the first thing they think is, "Is this really happening? Is this real? This must be a nightmare."

As the mother or father of an addict, this is what it feels like in their shoes: Let's say a mother is holding onto a rope, attached to a helicopter, hovering over the Grand Canyon. She is consumed with unbelievable terror and Dr. Phil is shouting from the sidelines as he holds his Starbucks Latte, "Don't fuck this up! If you make the wrong choice, your kid will die!" The wind is swinging her back and forth and if she lets go, goodbye mom. That kind of fear. The fear a parent feels when they know every minute of the day, their child may be dead in five minutes. That fear never lifts. It never leaves a parent's heart. All day long wondering when *it's* going to happen.

So, the list of rules for the stupid parents. You know what parents with young addicted kids do every morning? They walk to the kid's bedroom door and grab the handle, but they don't open the door. They stand there for a few minutes, with their hearts beating a thousand beats a minute, because they don't know what they will find. Will the love of their life be alive? What will they see when they open that door?

So. The rule book. Many parents know their child is using drugs in their home. Parents don't even need to read the shitty parent handbook to know that's a broken rule. But you know why they suck that up? Because when their kid is on death's doorstep, all they want to do is look at them. Study them. Notice exactly how their faces look when they smile. Desperately try to soak up the sound of their laughter. Listen to the sound of their voice. Because when they are gone, this mother and father will have only these sounds and images forever. These seconds will be their only comfort.

Mothers and fathers also think about what will happen to their own lives when their child is gone. What does that look like? What will they do? How will they survive? These are not thoughts of parents who do not have an addicted child. Because this is in their heads so much of the day, they do things like pulling out of a parking lot without seeing a car coming. They forget things. They sit at green lights. They feel a rush to their stomach when the phone rings. They don't sleep. They don't eat. They don't laugh. Then, again, they wonder, What am I going to do when my child is not here?

See, none of this is in the rule book. The rule book is missing the "heart" part. Because the bottom line is, death is death. And when it's your kid that is going to die, the method they use to get there doesn't matter. At all.

Another fact that is huge. Giant. Parents believe in their children, always. A parent's connection to their child is a rope that cannot be cut. The moment they are born, parents know for sure, their child is special. This child is much better than other children. Have you ever heard a parent with a week-old baby saying, "I can't believe how smart she is already." They really believe the infant is highly intelligent. They can clearly see it. No one else can, but don't tell the parents.

Parents spend their lives dumping as much support, love, and understanding on their child. If they are down, mom and dad lift them up. And they don't do this because it's in the good parent handbook. They do it because they love them with their entire hearts. They do it because they knew this kid was extraordinary at six days old. So when the professionals say, "Shut it down," it's not natural for parents to "arm's length" their children. The equivalent is to tell a parent to walk backwards for the rest of their lives. It's not natural.

No matter what they do, say, or believe, we have one hundred percent faith in our kids. So one of the rules in the book is that the built-in crazy love from a parent for their child is not useful. But the problem—useful or not—that's in our hearts. Forever.

Dr. Phil, these parents don't need to be demeaned and yelled at like they're children. They need a hug and a cup of tea and possibly a massage. Because no one knows how they would get through it until they are actually in it.

I know, "two sides to a pancake," "verbs in the sentences," you're "just an old country boy from Texas..." I know man. I know. But you are way off the reality of knowing what it's like to be a parent of an addicted child and the toll it takes on a parent's spirit. You have no idea. And it's not in the rule book.

Heaven

My mom told me a story when I asked if she ever had a big dream for her life. She told me that when she was about nineteen years old, one of the popular girls from her high school was getting married and that she wasn't invited to the wedding because she was not one of the "popular girls."

She ran into this girl and was so eager to attend this wedding, she told the girl she was a professional photographer and would be willing to take the wedding photos for free. I believe to this day, this was the only shady, edgy thing my mother ever did in her entire life. The bride was thrilled and mom was officially invited.

Mom went to the wedding excited to be involved in any way. She took her old, beat-down camera and began taking photos—bride and groom kissing, bride laughing throwing the bouquet, cute flower girl, the whole thing captured for the newly married couple to look back on with their grandchildren—until the man at the photo shop told her she took every photo with the lens cap on. Mom became even more unpopular and her only dream of being a professional photographer came crashing to a black, unfocused end. She finished the story about her dreams by saying, "And that was the end of that."

I have memories of being small enough to wrap my arms around my mother's leg, the feeling of her nylons.

This act was always to convey that I was throwing the gauntlet down. Whatever had happened, holding onto my mom's leg and staring at the offender until my mother demanded the perp give back the toy, the leg embrace was to show I knew people in high places. And when I say high, I mean tall.

If I had a nightmare, I would walk into my parent's room where my mom would see me, scoot, and lift the blanket. I would lie there with my mom's arm thrown over me, protecting me from the entire world. My parents never knew that I may have had one nightmare in all my ten years of life. I just preferred the sleeping arrangement.

My mother passed away June 29, 2014.

For whatever reason, I couldn't process it at all. I knew I wasn't myself. I was continually telling my husband and daughters, "I don't feel well." I didn't feel good. My brain was on delay. I couldn't remember things like how to get to the grocery store or my phone number or the spelling of simple words.

In my opinion, it's not the death part, but transition from here to there. There's nothing beautiful about watching someone you love die. There are the standard phrases that people use: "What a gift that you got to be there when she went to heaven."

Most of the comforting sayings involve the word "heaven" and how breathtaking and serene it is and how wonderful it is that she's there, encouraging me with their knowledge of all that heaven has to offer. Apparently, everything is soft and floating and colorful. I'm not comforted by the incessant references to heaven.

Yes, I believe my mother is in heaven, but the only person that benefits from heaven is the person that goes to heaven. The people left behind don't feel the relief or beauty, although, it may be just me. It's like if a friend called me from an Eagles concert in Hawaii. Yes, I'm sure it is lovely.

My mother had to have a D&C because she had an infection for about a year and she had become immune to antibiotics regardless of their strength. I believed she was having this surgery and then I would take her back to the nursing home. Two things were added to Mom's already staggering health problems. The first was that she would, from that day forward, need to use the restroom into a bag that would permanently hang from her wheelchair. The other new problem was that she could no longer swallow.

So she couldn't walk or talk, she was in a twenty-four-hour-a-day hallucination, the Parkinson's medication was not working anymore so she shook violently, she was immune to antibiotics, and now, she couldn't use the bathroom or swallow.

The oncologist recommended hospice, which I didn't know was even an option, and it caught me off guard. He said she would be taken off the medication she had been taking for the past twenty years and they would make her comfortable with morphine. The entire concept made my head swirl because I didn't anticipate it at all.

I was shocked he would use the word "hospice" because I had planned on taking her back to her room and watching her hallucinate and cry for the next ten years. He said because she didn't have something life-threatening like cancer, it would take a few months. A few months seemed less frightening.

Mom was lying in her hospital bed. On day three, I said, "Mom. We need to make a choice and I would feel better if you made it." Suddenly, she was more alert than I had seen in about five years, paying very close attention to what I was saying. "We have two different choices and whatever you want is what we will do. You can go back to the nursing home, but you will have to go to the restroom in this bag, and you are not going to be allowed solid food because you're not swallowing properly anymore." She was still focused on my words, "Or, you can go into hospice. You wouldn't have to take your Parkinson's medication and you would pass away like Dad did."

She answered immediately, "I don't want to go back. I want hospice."

It felt like the wrong answer.

I said, "Let's just sit on this for a few hours, okay?" I felt apprehensive and wondered if she understood what I was saying.

Mom took a nap and when she awoke, I asked again. Again she said she didn't want to go back. I asked if she understood that this would mean she would pass away, and she said she was ready.

I asked a few more times, because while Mom was ready, I didn't know if I was ready. Yes, she'd been very sick for very long, but how does someone make such a deliberate, permanent decision?

The nurse walked in with her Parkinson's medication and Mom said, "I don't want it."

The nurse knew about the decision to go to hospice and said, "Okay," and she threw it in the trash.

The hospice Mom was taken to was beautiful, gleaming with color and warmth. I told my husband, I would die there. The room was light brown, mustard yellow, and orange. Flowers and plants were scattered around. Comforting paintings covered the walls. It didn't reflect the purpose of this room, a place where people die, but I liked the attempt.

Day one of hospice, I had a nervous breakdown. Mom had been taken off her medications and she was lying in her bed crying, teeth chattering, moaning, her entire body writhing in agony. I lay next to her trying to hold her as tight as I could whispering, "It's okay, Mom. I love you. It's going to be okay."

After about fifteen minutes, I jumped up and ran down the hall toward the nurse in panic, "I made the wrong decision. Make this stop! Stop this! Make her the way she was! I did the wrong thing!" Apparently, hospice isn't reversible and the nurse, my daughter, and the doctor calmed me down. They doubled her morphine and that did put her to sleep.

Day three, the hospice pastor told me Mom was "active," a term used when a person is showing signs of passing away. I said, "But the doctor said it would take a few months?"

She said, "No, just a few days now." Well now I was thrown way off my mental plan and the confusion overwhelmed me. What? A few days? But he said a few months? What?

For the six days mom was in hospice, she was gasping for air. The fluid would build up in her throat and it sounded like she was drowning. After about four days of this, I had to wear my earbuds and never take them out because it's a natural instinct to try and help someone who is suffocating, especially your mother. What I remember most was the loud sound of Mom's labored breathing.

Hospice was described as being very peaceful and the morphine would make her fall into a peaceful sleep. That's how it happened with my father. He was asleep for days, and then he passed away.

It was nothing like what was happening with my mother. It was a horror show. This was the prayer I said every single day as I watched her struggle every second: "God. The last nine years have been really, really heartbreaking. Please just give her five seconds of relief. Five seconds of peace. It may not even be for her. It may be for me. Maybe I need to know that my mother had five seconds in her life where she wasn't struggling. Please, God, five seconds." I said that prayer every day, several times a day, for six days.

Mom had been in motionless coma, except for the gasping for air, for almost five days when I walked into her room. I saw some nurses and I saw my husband holding Mom's hand talking to her. He was saying, "Don't worry. I will take care of Dina and the kids. Everything will be fine." I walked closer and there lay my mother with her eyes wide, wide open, staring at my husband as he spoke.

I would love to say this was beautiful and touching, but when your mother opens her eyes really big after being in a coma, it's actually very scary. At least it was for me.

My husband continued, "It's okay for you to go with Ed" (my father). "Everyone here will be fine. We love you so much." I sat on the bed and held her hand and the color of her face seemed to change and look purplish. I thought she was dying right that second and it filled me with fear.

I wish I had responded better, but I didn't. I ran out of the room saying, "No! No!" I slumped on the floor in the hallway, now my eyes wide open. My feeling was, I know my mother is going to die, but I can't watch her die. My husband came out and collected me. By the time I got back in the room, mom was back in her coma, eyes closed.

Three days in the hospital, six days in hospice, the only day I slept at home was my birthday and then I was back at the hospice at five a.m. with my earbuds in, sleeping in a chair. The perpetual thought in my head was, But he said a few months!

The doctor said there was no medical explanation why mom was still alive. There is a study that someone did about people in hospice. They had found that often, people don't die in front of the people they love. They

IT WILL RAIN

recommended that I tell my mother I was going home for the day and also tell her not to wait for me. To go ahead and go with my father and it was okay to do that. So that's what I did.

I had been gone from the hospice for half an hour when my daughter, Jen, called and said, "It happened." Jen went in to see mom and told her she forgot her drink in the car. Jen went outside, got her drink, and mom passed away as Jen walked back into the room.

I once had a conversation with Mom about heaven and how exactly you get in. She never veered from what she believed: you give your life to Jesus, confess all your sins, and then try not to sin anymore.

I suggested it could be a numbers game, a system of points. You do a good thing, you get a point, and then you need "X" amount of points to get into heaven.

I've lived a life of being an active heathen. Over the past few years, though, I've been thinking I do want to go to heaven, but the "not sinning anymore" always trips me up because I'm habitual. So I'm putting all my faith in God and getting into heaven on the point system. But I'm in a situation where, for example, if I was in a math class at the end of the semester and I am failing. I'm having to do extra credit, get extra work. That's what is happening with my heaven points.

First, every time I do a good deed, I look up, to God, and I'm thinking in my head, You just saw that, right? Because when you're behind, the records need to accurate. Secondly, I don't have the luxury that high-point people have. I can't even walk past a piece of paper in a parking lot. I can't pretend that homeless person didn't ask me for change. I have to hold the door open. I have no choice. Point here, point there; I'll be in heaven in no time.

If you need a million points to get into heaven, my mother had seventy-five zillion. I'm guessing there's a "no-wait" line at the Pearly Gates for the high-point people. They would tell my mother, "Just come right in. Make yourself at home."

There are two scenarios that would enable me to go to heaven today. One is if my mother could roll over her unused points. Like frequent flier miles, although, it's easier to get into heaven than to actually use frequent flier miles.

The second is mom could say, "She's with me." Like a Studio 54 situation. Just slide me in under the red rope.

Or, I guess I could stop sinning, but that's hard.

I drove back to Mom's hospice and sat next to my mother. The people in the room left so I could have a minute alone with her. I lay my head on her chest and it was so cold, the realness of it stunned me. I didn't know that happened so quickly and that memory goes through my head still.

In the first writing of this, I omitted something because of my desperate need to be liked and approved of. When the coldness of my mother's chest startled me, I quickly lifted my head. I looked down and whispered, "I am fucking livid."

I was angry because God didn't answer my prayer. I don't know if that was the wrong reaction or right reaction, but that's what I said. That's what I felt. Of course looking back, I wish I had been stronger and said something really inspiring.

I held my mother's hand and said, "You will have peace in your new life. I loved you more than you could possibly know. Thank you for being my mother."

It's common for my grandson, Matt, to come running to me and wrap his arms around my leg looking for a way out of trouble. For those seconds, Matt feels it's me and

IT WILL RAIN

him against the world. He knows he can't lose as long as he's wrapped around my leg. It's automatic protection. It's family history.

One day, I will feel the beauty in all of it. It was powerful. It was painful. My mother was the kindest human being in the world and, at the exact same time, she was the strongest person I have ever known. I need redemption. I need healing. I guess I just need some time.

And that was the end of that.

Little Cakes

When I was a child, I remember one Christmas we were doing a performance of the Christmas pageant, the musical stage play about the birth of Jesus.

I was really excited about my part, even though it was the only non-speaking part in the play. I believe the actual character was written on the script as "walking child," and I had practiced ahead of time for weeks. All I had to do was carry a chalice that had pretend wine in it down the center aisle of the church and set it on the altar. And then walk back. That was my part.

I decided instead of just walking, I would put one foot forward, and then I would bring the other foot to the stretched out foot. Then I would use the opposite foot to step forward and bring the other foot up to that foot. Sort of like the Waltz, but with no partner and in a straight line. If I did it as I rehearsed it, it would take twenty minutes to walk up and back. The entire play lasted about thirty minutes and my walking part would take up twenty.

Right before I was about to blow their minds, my nose began to bleed. Then I fainted. So they grabbed some kid wearing a vest and shiny black shoes out of the audience and said, "Take this chalice and go set it on the altar."

The rage made my nose bleed more because this amateur, random kid was stealing—let's face it—the role of a lifetime. Not just anyone could be "walking child."

I watched this bullshit from the back stage kitchenette and I was fuming as I sat there with a bloody tissue against my nose. After the show I heard this kid's parents tell him, "Great job, sweetie! We're so proud of you!" I was glaring at him with blood on my dress.

On the way home, my parents told me not to worry, I could do it next year. Next year? Next year I want a goddamn speaking part, Mom and Dad. My mom was wiping the plastic seat with a tissue as my nose was still bleeding, "Hold your head up, Dina!" wiping up the blood and my shattered dreams.

One Christmas I got an Easy-Bake oven. That was the year I realized that I was going to get the shaft for the rest of my life.

The Easy-Bake oven came with ONE cake mix and forty years ago, they didn't sell them separately, so you would bake one miniature cake—done. It's over. The toy is no longer fun. There is no other function for it.

I tried to make it into a Barbie house, which is what I actually wanted. I would pretend it was their hotel. I laid them on the mini cake rack. Then took them off the rack. I took the actual rack out and then the Barbies could sit in there like they were on a bus trip or sitting and chatting while they waited to get mammograms. I took a plastic Barbie pump and put it in the oven with the hope I could watch it melt. It wasn't even hot enough to melt the pump. All of the activities above took about ten minutes.

It took about sixty seconds to eat my little cake and since it was raw in the middle, I had to spit it into a paper towel.

My brothers saw my disappointment so they pounced like starving wolverines, "Hey Dina! Why don't you make us a cake?" Laughing and laughing. "We're starving!

IT WILL RAIN

Bake us something!" And there they sat, with their brand-spanking-new chemistry sets.

I responded quickly, "Fuck off." I was ten.

I grew up in Albuquerque, New Mexico. One house we lived in was a little house on a dirt road with an acre of land between each house. Barbed wire separated each property, although, we didn't own the land on either side.

It was the first and only house we ever lived in that had a washing machine inside. Not a washer AND a dryer, but a washer. Then we would hang the wet clothing on the clothesline in the backyard.

Everything we had in our house was rigged with something to make the thing work. Televisions always had wire clothes hangers shoved in holes in the back, positioned to get, at best, a fuzzy picture. If someone walked by the television, the picture would become static with black and white lines.

The washing machine was also rigged. It had a big, black, hard plastic tube that went from the back of the washing machine through a hole hand-cut through the back door and then stretched out into a field behind the house. So the water would come out of the back of the washer and go through the tube and into the field.

UNLESS, it was really cold.

In that scenario, we would all be whittling or folk dancing, and hear a flood of water coming back into the house because the tube was frozen causing the water to backtrack. People would come running from all directions in the house to turn off the washing machine, but by that time, most of the floor was under about an inch of water.

My bedroom was also the living room or common area of the house. I had just turned eighteen and I had my baby in her crib in the middle of the house. People would walk through "my room" to get to other parts of the house like the bathroom or kitchen, so there was plenty of traffic. I would see people walking my direction and put my finger up to my lips, "Shhhh! Did you not see a teen with her infant trying to sleep on a bed in the middle of the living room? Damn man."

Because of the location, my room was right next to the elegant laundry room, so I was usually the first one to hear the flooding of the washing machine. I would run as fast as I could, pull the "off" knob as the water rolled over my feet. Then we mopped the floor for about three hours. And when I say mop, I exaggerate. We didn't have a mop. We used towels that would now need to be washed.

It was a system meant to break us and kick our asses every single day. There was always a pile of soaking wet towels sitting by the washing machine to remind us that we were God's least favorite people.

So if the Lord Jesus Christ had mercy on our souls and we could actually wash a load of clothes, we would then hang them on the clothesline in the backyard—another challenge. Winter in New Mexico can be really, really cold. So when you went out later that day to remove the dry clothing, not only would they not be dry, they would be frozen solid.

You could stand a pair of Levi's straight up and lean them against a wall. The only way to dry the clothing in the winter would be to lay them on chairs, tables, and couches all over the house—wet, frozen clothing everywhere.

It was common to eat a bowl of cereal in the "V" of the armpit of a shirt lying on the kitchen table. When you sat on the couch, most of the time, your back rested on drying towels or jeans.

When I was a kid, I really didn't have a clue we were hillbilly gypsies until one Christmas. My mom and I were in a Goodwill store. My mother picked up a little brown

IT WILL RAIN

stuffed animal puppy. She said, "Oh! This is cute, don't you think?"

I looked at it, "Yeah. Who's that for?" She said it's for the "needy" people. I thought, poor needy people, because it had a huge shit stain right on its back.

Christmas morning I woke up, opened my gift—a brown, shit-stained dog. I thought, Holy shit! We ARE the needy people! I prayed my disappointment didn't show as my mother watched me open the gift. It was a confirmation that we were poor. I hadn't noticed it before, even as I lifted my leg to watch my television show. I thought everyone lived this way.

I was also shocked to know that even when poor people walk in to the Goodwill store, they say, "It's fun to look around 'these stores.'" As if we didn't belong there or we were somehow *above* the store, and now I find out on Christmas morning that we blend in at the Goodwill store. The Goodwill store was created for people like us. I was livid, and uncomfortable in my wet jeans, as I looked at the shit-stained dog.

I had that stuffed dog for a long time because I felt sorry for my mom having to be one of the needy people. I pretended this dog was very important to me to make my mom happy. I carried it from every house or room that I moved to.

I was in my living room/bedroom with my baby when I heard the flooding water rushing back into the house from the frozen black tube. I jumped up, slammed the newborn under my armpit and ran like an elk through the water to quickly pull the knob.

I stood there out of breath and still, infant under my arm, and in slow-motion, I turned my head and saw the water rushing down the steps into my living room/bedroom, making its way across the floor where shit-stained puppy was tucked in a corner.

I began to run, baby literally in one hand. I leaped, trying to beat the water and save Goodwill dog's life. By the time I got there, my shit-stained dog was soaking wet. I put it on a window ledge outside so it would dry, frozen solid.

There's only so much compassion I can have for my mother. I had taken all I could. I threw it away and vowed that I would never buy my children toys from the Goodwill. Little. Did. I. Know. I have repeated the line, "These stores are fun to look around in!" more times than I can count.

I complain about my life. I have a washer and dryer and a mop that I rarely use. We don't have any money, but our "not having any money" is much different than my parents' "not having any money."

My parents not having any money meant living in complete darkness. I mean, we didn't have electricity—that kind of dark. I remember hearing my father's voice in the darkness telling my brother, "Kevin. Go outside and see if the neighbors have lights." The neighbors always had lights.

I know that for my parents to provide Christmas for six children had to be very stressful. I understand and have compassion now that I'm old. I get it.

John and I have always managed to get the expensive gifts even when we couldn't afford them. Then, because of the financial stress, we were shitting blood for a few months. But the kids were happy and that's what matters, right?

One day, my daughters will shit blood for their children. It's the circle of life.

Happy Ending

Depression feels like walking through a dark room that never gets light. Holding my arms out, moving them back and forth to avoid running into a wall or a door, and scooting my feet across the floor so I don't trip on a toy or a book. That bit of fear until my hand finally rests against the wall.

I can follow the wall to the door, still feeling unsure, but knowing from memory the door is there. But where is it? Why is it taking so long to get there, turn the handle, see the light, and feel some relief? The wall goes on and on and I walk forever looking for the door. My breathing is labored as I pray someone—anyone—will open the door and set me free.

But they don't because they don't know I haven't seen the light for eight months. That I've been trapped in complete darkness and I can't find my way out. They don't know I am lost.

But if I found the door, I could crack it open just enough for the light to peek through and I could save myself. I could find my way out. I could make the light brighter.

The other night as I turned off all the lights in the house to walk to my bedroom, I didn't have a second thought. The house was pitch black as I glided through rooms and doorways with complete confidence, like an ice skater, sliding my hand down the hallway wall not caring how long the journey was, just knowing I would get there.

Walking into my bedroom, I closed the door almost dancing over the cars and trucks my grandson littered around the floor. Finally getting to my bed, scooting the dog over and lying still in the darkness, I was thankful for how far I've come. Thankful that I'm still here. Thankful that I can move through the darkness with faith and hope because now I know for sure the darkness is connected to the light. From now on I'm going to remember that. The darkness is always connected to the light.

I am not a doctor or an expert on depression or any other emotional conditions. I can only share my experience and what worked for me. Depression kills people. It's a dangerous medical condition. Long before a physical death, there is a spiritual, emotional death that the people around you can't see.

What worked, in my experience, were the annoying suggestions to "do something." Get dressed, get out, breathe the outside air, walk, do everything you can to stay out of your bed. That is the answer. Act "as if." Act as if you feel better, even if you don't feel better.

Throughout my life I have been very close to every different kind of person, people with different beliefs and different levels of intelligence, rich people and poor people. I know people who have stocked canned goods and bottled water as they wait for the "rapture" and I also know many atheists.

Most things about life confuse me, but occasionally, I look at the big things in life and wonder why we make it so difficult and confusing. I think about God, believing in God or not believing in God. Then we add the textbooks, and everyone splits up, and they go to different structures where they all have the same textbook.

Each structure has a list of rules to follow. One group says you can do this thing, but the structure next door says you can't do that thing. There are special days throughout the year and, depending on the structure, these days can be expensive or they may be just another day. Special days may involve candles, eggs, presents, eating large quantities of food, or eating no food at all.

The people in some structures pray quietly with their heads bowed, while the people in other structures pray loudly, shouting, waving their arms in the air (like they just don't care). Some places have a set-up for kids, equipped with kid's textbooks for coloring, and other places make the kids sit still and quiet, which they will never do even if Jesus wants them to.

In my opinion, all the above is fine. Good. Great. If you find comfort and happiness in the structure, awesome.

A very beautiful friend of mine said she didn't believe in God and she used the line that I have used and I have heard hundreds of times: "There is no proof God exists."

For me, just me, God is like a feeling. God is like love. If I said I love my husband, someone could say, "Put the love you feel for your husband in this cup." I couldn't do it. It's something that's in my heart. Love is not a thing. I can't prove my love exists by showing evidence, or scientific research, or providing the textbooks that say the feeling of love in my heart is true and real. When I love someone, I feel love in my heart. I don't have proof.

God is the same. If I say a prayer to God, I feel calm and safe. I can't put that safe, serene feeling in a box so that you can peek inside and see with your own eyes that what I feel in my heart is real.

God is a feeling in my heart. I can't prove God exists, but I can say that when I pray, that feeling—that connection—helps me to keep going down the street. I carry the proof of God in my heart, but it's not something I can show you in the palm of my hand. I don't know how I can prove God is in my heart, just like I don't know how I can prove love is in my heart.

There are people that don't believe in God because of the structures and the rules and the beliefs of the competing groups. Some of these structured groups do a huge disservice to God. People run away from God screaming, and I don't blame them.

One thing I am positive about is that "God" and "the structure" are not the same thing. God is in the hearts of the people in the structure, yet God has nothing to do with the rules or the beliefs. People make up the rules and the rules are in place because of the textbook they are given after they learn the secret handshake.

I think the smartest thing to do is to take all the above and make up your own mind. If you want a textbook, get one. If you want to go to the structure because you have good friends and family who go there, great. If you want to stay at home and have God there with you, also great. Hide the eggs, or don't. Give the presents, or not. Refuse food and water, or eat a turkey and drink wine.

I know for sure that you can have God walk with you every day and you don't even have to tell anyone. You can feel comfort in knowing you are never alone. You can have rules or not. The only thing you should try to do is just do what's good—that's all—do what's right. I guess that's actually a rule, but that's a rule whether you believe in God or not.

Every day I eat, drink, sleep, shower, work, and I talk to God. The words I say to God every single night are: "Thank you, God, for my husband, my daughters, my grandsons, and my mother." Every night the same prayer for years.

IT WILL RAIN

I can't put happy in a cup. I can't put love in a cup. I can't put God in a cup. But these things are there every day for me. Or you. Or not. Whatever.

When I would visit my mother in the nursing home, I searched for value in the visit. I know there is value in every human being. There is always something to learn. So I listened and watched, praying she would say something that reminded me that this person was my mother.

When I looked at my mom, I was crushed to see her watch these people on the religious channel, people that had clearly been given so much, and I wondered why God gave my mom nothing? She prayed all day long every day. And she couldn't get one single break?

In my head, I can see my mother's hands and remember all the babies she'd held, all the hugs she had given to so, so many people. I can see right now in my head the thousands of times I had seen my mom's hands raised in worship during a church service. She spent the last ten years of her life being terrorized by violent hallucinations twenty-four hours a day, seven days a week. Really?

What if I never get the answers about my mom being robbed. Can I accept that I may never have the answer? Because I'm realizing now, I don't think I will ever get a solid answer. I have to accept that. It's between Mom and God, and I have no choice but to accept it.

Then I had a huge realization about my mom. I thought my mom's life sucked because she never did anything. She never dreamed about doing some great thing and then went out and tried to do it.

I've always had some kind of dream that I am actively working on. Always. Mom didn't, so I always felt her life was small and miserable. Then something hit me like a ton of bricks. All my mother ever wanted was to be married to my dad and have her children. That *was* her dream. That was all she wanted. She wanted to go to church, and pray, and laugh, and have her husband and children. That's not a small life. That's a content, full, peaceful life.

That's the kind of life you live when you stay on the path God planned for you. Just loving the people God sent to you. What a powerful statement that is for me and all the rest of us who are running on the mouse wheel to make dreams come true. Happiness is standing right in front of us and that's the reason for our life.

Our dreams are a side show, not the main event. I have always had that backwards. I was wrong. She was right all along.

I'm a huge fan of setting boundaries. But I'm a bigger fan of apologizing the next day for setting a boundary. The experts said I needed to let the people I loved go so they could learn and grow and become amazing or not. I was all for it as long as I was completely entangled in every aspect of their lives so I could stop them right before they slammed into a wall. My words and actions were actually powerful enough to save my daughters' lives.

I took the position that whatever horrible thing one of them said or did, if I loved them more, they would stop doing stupid things. If I hugged them, kissed them, lifted them up *more*, they would stop. It didn't matter how horrible the actions or words were. If they took a swing at me, told me I was a horrible mother, ran their vehicle into my house, more love would make it stop.

There have been people who believe I have enabled my daughters. I would agree, but secretly, I thought the person giving me this information didn't love their children nearly as much as I loved mine. I love my daughters much more than any other mother.

I also thought I was more intelligent than other people in the same predicament. I knew if I could just find the magic words and say them in the exact, right tone, the power of my words would hit the kid in just the right way and their life would be saved.

I spent fifteen years making sure the girls never hit the concrete, always grabbing them with seconds to spare.

You can set boundaries all day long, but if you don't enforce them, it is only a suggestion. In my extremely limited experience with boundaries, even the mention of them makes people irate. That is exactly why I never enforced them.

I had the same problem saying "no." I was unable to say no, ever, for any reason. The constant thread in every conflict was that I was a shitty mom. I had made some big, huge mistakes, so my privilege of setting boundaries was permanently revoked.

Most of the time, I would jump through hoops just so I didn't have to have the "you were a shitty mother" conversation. But it seemed the moment I jumped through one hoop, there would be another waiting. And another. And another. It never ended.

So I would set a boundary and then take it back. I would say no and then say yes. I would let them go and then take them back.

I would orchestrate a ceremony of sorts, always lighting something on fire, Native American music playing throughout. Or dramatically post a piece of paper with the new boundary written in bold letters on a heavy traffic wall. Nothing worked. At one point, I decided to simply stop speaking. No one noticed. I finally set a solid boundary with the girls and they curiously didn't even flinch. I said, "I want my life back. Your problems are yours. Peace." They acted relieved. What?

So now I wonder, all the years of helping and standing by their sides through all the trials and hardships, did they ever even ask for that? Was I inserting myself into their lives and making it impossible for them to grow? Did they ever really need me to take care of their lives? Was I not as brilliant and powerful as I thought I was? This is terrible. And shocking.

There have been a few attempts at ignoring the boundary, and I always put an immediate halt to it. And guess what. They are still alive. Sorry about the childhood! It's like the old saying about motherhood, "Do the time. Don't let the time do you."

There wasn't a particular day that I woke up and said, "Oh. I'm not depressed anymore." I lived my life and then one day I looked back over the last several months and realized that I was feeling better. I looked out my kitchen window and said to myself, "Wow. I feel better. I'm bordering on feeling great. How did that happen?" It happened with time—time and movement.

I do believe, for sure, that doing the little things I didn't want to do, like getting out of bed, getting dressed, getting my hair done, going to dinner with my family, these things pushed me to feel better.

At one point during my depression, I decided I needed to have a weekly activity that forced me out of the house. I had not been in school since I dropped out of high school in ninth grade. I decided to take a creative writing class.

Getting out of the truck and walking to the admissions office to make this happen was exhausting. I could hardly lift my legs. I was pale and had dark circles under my eyes. As I passed the twenty-year-olds I thought, What am I doing? But I did it and went to my class the following week.

I was not only older than all of the students, I was older than the teacher. But, I did it. I turned in every assignment and did not miss one class. Are you ready for this? I got an A-plus. Thirteen A-pluses to be exact.

So day-by-day, week-by-week, I got my inside stuff back—my faith, hope, and laughter. It didn't just come flooding back. Just a piece here and a piece there.

There have been several occasions I think back to the night that I took a handful of pills and woke up in the psych ward. What if it would have happened? What if my suicide attempt actually killed me?

That would've been horrible. Because since that day, there has been laughter, tears, joy, chocolate, movies, pasta, and more laughter. More times than I can count, I have been spilling over with love and real happiness. Ending my life would have been disastrous and I would have missed everything.

My fourteen-year-old grandson, Moses, has cerebral palsy and autism. He is finally in a school and an after-school program that fit his disabilities perfectly. At six o'clock at night, the first time he rode the United Cerebral Palsy bus home from his after-school program, the bus driver opened the bus door and there sat my Moses. He was smiling and happy, and he was surrounded by beautiful children who were exactly like him. Finally, Moses was not different.

I helped him off the bus as several children yelled, "Bye Moses!" He smiled and waved goodbye and continued to wave at the bus as it traveled all the way down our street and turned the corner out of sight.

April and Moses are a team, and watching April be a mom to a child with disabilities, and doing it with such grace and unending love, is inspiring. My handsome grandson Moses has become a young man. I love them both.

Jennifer is also an amazing mom to my four-year-old grandson, Matthew. Matt speaks AA lingo. I can ask him a question, he will answer the question and then say, "Thank you for listening."

I say, "Hey, Matt. I don't want you to be up on the counter like that."

Matt says, "I'm happy with myself and life right now. Thank you."

When I met John twenty-seven years ago, I had two small daughters. So we have literally never been alone. Now, all three of the girls are off living their lives and doing a great job of navigating the world. I'm proud of the way they turned things around. And John and I are alone. All alone. And it's glorious, it just is.

I still have moments when my heart is suddenly filled with sadness and I feel immediate fear. I feel the crackle of thunder and think, is this the beginning of another year in bed? Am I going to be making a log cabin out of Popsicle sticks in the psych ward by tomorrow? Then I cry for seven seconds and it's gone. But the feeling of sadness is rare, very rare.

I know of people in my life that have succeeded in committing suicide. Sitting where I am today, relaxed and happy, I feel like possibly, all of these people would have gotten to the other side if they could have held on. But that's the struggle, right? Holding on.

I know on most days just breathing in and out takes every ounce of energy you have. I know some days it's actually painful to breathe in and out. I know you're saying you don't have any real reason to stick around. But if you just breathe in and out for as long as you can, then breathe longer, at some point a reason will present itself. It is an absolute fact. It will happen. I know it takes a mountain of strength to ride that out, but I believe we all have that strength. I believe in you.

If you hold on, I promise you the payoff is huge. Because when you've been that low and heartbroken for that long and the sun finally comes out, your appreciation for every single thing in your life is multiplied by a thousand.

Normal people could not possibly see the world with such brilliant color because they have not lived in the dark. Everything in your life becomes brighter, sweeter, and funnier.

So would I rather have never experienced this horrific depression and see the world in pastel coloring like everyone else? To be honest, yes I would. I would rather have never spent eight months in my pajamas lying in my bed. Pastel is not horrible, but that's not the way it worked out.

So I will embrace the bright blue, purple, green, and yellow, and know that most people can't even see it. I can see it very clearly.

Combat Boots

I had a dream about five months into my stay in bed. There was a little girl standing in the desert. She had blonde hair and was wearing a dress and boots. Not girly boots, but combat boots. I couldn't really make out her face.

She was standing still and then it began to get windy. The wind started to blow and the dirt was blowing all over this child. She shielded her face with her arms as her hair and dress blew around. Then the wind stopped. She stood there.

It began to rain. She again shielded herself from the rain as it fell soaking her from head to toe. Then the rain stopped. Again, she stood there.

Then the bright sun came out. She looked up at the sun with her hair and dress still wet. She looked down at her dress and I could see her grabbing up the bottom of her dress and wringing out the water, then smoothing out the dress. Then she looked back up at the sun. Then I woke up.

I still remember that dream. It was so vivid. It seemed like a simple, interesting little dream when I thought about it later that day. But the more I thought about it after my depression went away, the more it intrigued me.

It was an example of the seasons of life. My depression was just a season in my life. It's a piece of my life—not my whole life.

I am that little girl wringing out my dress, wearing combat boots. I'm ready for more sun and less rain.

A Letter to Me

You walked in a whole person and walked out in pieces. The memory you've been trying to remove from your head for thirty-six years—I want you to know that you were just a child and that day was not about you, but about the pain of the adults around you.

Sometimes, the people who are supposed to protect us simply get it wrong. They make huge mistakes. Huge. You will understand that when you grow up and you are responsible for protecting your own children and you make huge mistakes.

You were a young girl when you walked in that door and when you walked back out, you were a different person. Looking down at your feet, looking at the concrete, and feeling numb and invisible. You felt at that moment that you were not loved or valued as much as other people.

The young girl that was there just hours before was gone. The path that God carved specially for you was now a million miles away.

So you put all these feelings in a bag and walked down the road for thirty-six years. Invisible and unworthy.

You spent your life trying to shake the memory out of your head because the pain it would bring would be unbearable.

We all think by pretending it didn't happen, it will go away. But it doesn't go away. The pain you carry gets heavier and heavier and as you get older, the weight on your heart and your spirit is too great. So if you take the day, or days, you're trying to pretend never happened, then make a list of your fears, character flaws, and the things that make you feel vulnerable, and put the day and the list side-by-side, I think you will be shocked at the parallels. You believe you are over it and it has not affected your life, but why is the list so accurate and directly from that experience? Without realizing it, you are actually living that day every day.

It's good to be strong. But with some events, the description of being strong is being fragile and hurt and embracing that. It takes a ton of strength to be weak and accept weakness. We don't need to be strong every day, all day. People tell us that is what we need, but part of strength is being strong enough to be sad and hurt and go ahead and cry and break some stuff.

You will realize the key to your life is getting back on that path that God made just for you. No one stays on the path all the time. Everyone steps off or even walks away only to return because that's the place where you are most authentic and at peace.

I left you behind because that was the only way I could survive. God was never, ever disappointed with you. God has always been proud of you.

We have to recreate that day. You have to walk out that door, take my hand and lift your head. Together we will be strong enough to walk away in one piece.

Now I'm much stronger and much smarter, and I can see you sparkling in the night sky like a diamond, side-by-side with other people who got left behind. Other people who also feel invisible, but in reality, we all light up the sky with brilliant, beautiful color.

IT WILL RAIN

I will carry you in my heart down the road because you are loved. You are absolutely the best part of me. Let it go and be free.

ALSO BY DINA KUCERA:

Everything I Never Wanted To Be:
a memoir of alcoholism and addiction,
faith and family, hope and humor.

Made in the USA
Middletown, DE
12 June 2015